God's Mercies after Suicide: Blessings Woven through a Mother's Heart

Jean Ann Williams

Cover photo by James D. Williams
Cover design by Nina Newton, CreativeLife Publishing
Edited by Nina Newton, CreativeLife Publishing

God's Mercies after Suicide: Blessings Woven through a Mother's Heart
Copyright © 2016 by Jean Ann Williams
Published by Love Truth
www.joshua-mom.blogspot.com/

ISBN 978-0-9977016-1-6
Suicide – Death – Grief – Inspirational – Devotional

Printed in the United States of America

In memory of Joshua, a victim of suicide.
November 27, 1978–March 16, 2004

To my husband, and my children, Jami and Jason. Your loss has been great, yet you've encouraged me to lean on the Father of Life. With deepest gratitude, our family would like to thank those who prayed for us in the early grieving years. Your petitions on our behalf gave us the courage to walk through the valley of the shadows.

Acknowledgements

I'd like to thank the following people:

Pat Luffman Rowland for approaching me with the idea for this book of devotions, her encouragement, and for writing the first draft of the Preface. Susie Neal for her never ending faith in me, and her editorial suggestions early on. Susanne Lakin for her editorial skills. Opal Campbell and her perfect instincts in creating a fantastic book trailer. Nina Newton for her creative talents in the publishing process: book cover, graphics, a beautiful ad in her magazine, *Ruby for Women*, and her patience with me as we brought this book before readers.

Most of all, I give thanks to the Lord and my Savior, Jesus Christ. If it were not for You, I could not have written this story about loss, grief, and hope.

~ Jean Ann Williams

What people are saying about
God's Mercies after Suicide:

"In this stirring memoir Jean Ann Williams shares her son Joshua's life and also his untimely death at age twenty-five. Being a woman of faith, in each chapter she shares thoughts and Scriptures which have given her comfort and support in hopes her journey can help others. The book is a must read for anyone who has lost a family member to suicide."

—GLORIA HORSLEY Ph.D.
President of Open to Hope

"Jean Ann Williams has written a powerful book, full of pain and joy, despair and hope, all in the form of short, pithy devotions. This author understands the agony of losing someone to suicide, because her son took his life and shredded his family's heart. However, though Williams clearly spells out the agonizing grief she endured after her beloved son's death, she also shows God truly does offer a Light at the end of the long, dark tunnel of loss.

And as the author takes us on this long journey out of overwhelming darkness, she also enables us to feel the everlasting arms underneath her, carrying her and healing her every step of the way. If you or someone you know has lost a loved one through suicide, please get this book. It will bless and minister to you as often as you read one of its devotions or reflect on the words within its pages."

—KATHI MACIAS, (www.kathimacias.com)
is a multi-award winning author of more than 50 books.
She lives in Southern California with her husband Al.

"Jean Ann Williams provides a transparent account of the emotions and challenges surrounding the suicide death of her son, Josh. Reality, interspersed with memories, creates an accurate look at the difficulties inherent in suicide grief. But *God's Mercies after Suicide* also affords readers the opportunity to explore their own emotions and struggles and document their journey through the healing process."

—CANDY ARRINGTON, *AFTERSHOCK:*
Help, Hope, and Healing in the Wake of Suicide
(B & H Publishing Group)

CONTENTS

Preface

"The hard place in which you perhaps find yourself, so painful and bewildering, is the very place in which God is giving you opportunity to look only to Him, to travail in prayer, and to learn long-suffering, gentleness, meekness--in short, to learn the depths of love that Christ Himself has poured out on all of us."

~ Elisabeth Elliot, from *Keep a Quiet Heart*, p. 233
—Ephesians 1:7-8

Remember not the former things, nor consider the things of old. Behold, I am doing a new thing; now it springs forth, do you not perceive it? I will make a way in the wilderness and rivers in the desert.

—Isaiah 43:18–19

I had a dream the nightmare never happened. Our son, Joshua, never passed on to the hereafter. He married and had children. Then I woke and knew. *We live with our reality.*

I've written these devotions for mothers who have shared the deep heartache of a child's suicide.

Through my writing, I believe God wants me to share from my heart to yours, by encouraging and giving you ways to cope.

Hope and peace are possible after a suicide. God has helped me, and He wants to help others. The loss is horrific, but God is faithful. He brought me through this dark time, and He wants the same for you.

A yearning to write this book of devotions came five years after my loss of Joshua. I sensed God's strength within me, but I hadn't come this far in a blink.

As I wrote this true account, the Lord God's hand touched me and His Holy Spirit filled me with His peace.

God, when I faltered, You renewed my strength. Through Jesus, I came before You with these words, scriptures, and prayers for Your Glory, Amen.

7

ONE: March 16, 2004

You will not fear the terror of night, nor for the arrow that flies by day.

—Psalm 91:5

I stood in Joshua's open doorway.

With his hand on the inside of his bedroom doorknob, my twenty-five-year-old son, Joshua, bent down and reached for something on the bed.

For several years he declined emotionally. After trying several antidepressants, nothing worked and he became paranoid. My mother's heart feared all was not right.

Until this morning, I never understood what Joshua was considering.

Still clutching the knob, my son stood and faced me. His eyes met mine. He swung his arm and handed me his Bible. Our fingertips brushed, his lingering, lingering.

Solemn determination masked his face.

My stomach clenched by an invisible fist, as Joshua shut the door.

Turning the locked doorknob, it resisted. I called out Joshua's name.

A muffled shot.

Time slowed with the swish-swishing pulse in my ears. Why is Joshua shooting a starter pistol in his bedroom?

But, I understood on a heart level what my son had done.

I rushed in.

My son
        was

                    falling,
                                    falling, to his bed.

Reaching him, I shouted, "No, Joshua, no!"

Pressing my fingers on the wound at the side of his head, with my other hand I felt a pulse at Joshua's neck.

One beat.

Half a beat.

The skin of my fingers met the hush of his heart.

My eyes shut, facing upward I wailed, "Oh, God, please, no!"

A Mother's Memories

God knew I longed to have a third child, and yet I wasn't blessed to carry another to full term for six years.

At over three months' gestation with Joshua, I hemorrhaged.

His tiny self was determined to come too soon.

Up from my bed,

> down on my knees.

> I begged God for one

> more baby.

I rose from kneeling and my flow stopped.

This is the God I knew and loved.

I prayed, "Father, if this child is a daughter, her name will be Joy. In Jesus, I thank You, Amen."

Father, I'm amazed at how fast You answered my urgent prayer. You knew this child would not make it if I did not request Your powers to heal. You are a God of mercy. Through Jesus's holiness, Amen.

~Your Mother Memories~

~Your Prayer of Praise~

~A Scripture of Encouragement~

TWO: Within Two Hours

Be merciful unto me, O God, be merciful unto me: for my soul trusteth in thee: yea, in the shadow of thy wings will I make my refuge, until these calamities be overpast.

—Psalm 57:1 KJV

This mother's body trembled. *What could I have done better to keep him here? Would Joshua go to heaven?*

Emergency workers moved in the background. A few tight-knit family members stood in our living room in shocked silence.

I felt dead, as dead as my son in the next room. My adult daughter Jami knelt before me at the leather sofa. Tears streamed over her flushed face. "Mommy, I'm grateful you and Daddy are safe."

Safe?

Her brother, Joshua, lay in the other room. His body rested on the bed. His soul? It had flown to eternity.

The room hummed with a mixture of family and the authorities.

A voice scowled. "*Now* where is your God?"

Satan. I shuddered with terror. Another shock. A spiritual aftershock.

Similar, yet not, as when my son's heartbeat stuttered—*Good-bye, bye.*

My spirit flew into His arms of safety. My whole being chanted, *Jesus, Jesus, Jesus.*

Father, hold me. Let this daughter sob in Your rest. Your feathers * *cover me. Through Christ's precious name, I ask, Amen.*

---

* Psalm 91:4

A Mother's Memories

Born in Lindsay, California, on November 27, 1978, making us a family of five, my son, Joshua, came into the world with coal-black eyes and a shock of dark, feather-hair to match.

The first time the nurse brought him to me, cleaned and bundled, I gripped him around his chest and raised him as an offering to our God.

"He lives because of You, Lord."

I peered into my little one's face and began sing-songing, "Hi, Son."

His head stayed upright above strong baby neck muscles, his eyes zinged straight to mine.

"Hi, Son."

Baby Joshua swallowed, listening.

Mother and son bonded.

Thank You, Father, for giving me this long-awaited child. I'm blessed. In the name of Jesus, Amen.

~Your Mother Memories~

~Your Prayer of Praise~

~A Scripture of Encouragement~

THREE: A Short Time Later

I shall go to him, but he will not return to me.

—2 Samuel 12:23

"Jean." As I sat on our sofa, someone from across the room spoke my name.

The gurney, with Joshua's body hidden inside a black bag, rolled from the hall and into our living room. The young men attending paused.

I stood.

Their eyes grew wide as they watched me, mother of Joshua.

The men bowed their heads and rolled my son toward the front door.

I reached Joshua before anyone could stop me. "Wait!"

Sobs came from the steps at the opened back door. My daughter leaned into her husband's protective arms, her hands covering her face.

Doesn't Jami want to say good-bye?

Joshua's dog Heinrich sat Jami's feet.

Pulling my gaze from them, I unzipped the bag to expose Joshua's now peaceful and gentle face.

"Good-bye, my son."

Bending forward, my lips caressed his forehead.

"I'll love you forever." I kissed his warm lips.

One of the attendants zipped Joshua's death bag. It crackled shut.

No, no, no! I'm not done.

15

The gurney wheels stumbled over the threshold of the open front door. At the sound of its rattle, my soul shattered into a zillion pieces.

My knees dropped to the floor.

Hands grabbed and settled me on the sofa. I choked on my sobs, not able to catch a full breath, and my throat burned raw.

A soothing feminine voice, "She's getting too hot." A cool cloth pressed at my cheeks.

My daughter tipped a glass to my lips. "Mommy. Please, drink this."

Water? Nothing could quench the thirst for my lost son.

We cannot bear this horror, dear Lord. Hold us. Oh, I know You're here, God. Hold on to us!

A Mother's Memories

I enjoyed giving my first two babies lots of cuddling. With Joshua, I showed affection in the same way.

Having had problems with milk fever after each birth, I nursed our first two children only for a short time. When Joshua was born, the doctor prescribed a new medication for milk fever which would not ruin my milk. And so, I was able to nurse for much longer.

This became a blessing on many levels, for my little boy suffered from numerous illnesses. The nourishment Joshua took from me sustained him. He became plump and even appeared on the outside as a healthy baby.

As Joshua grew into a toddler, he showed affection by patting my cheek and saying, "Ah, baby."

Before bedtime each night, I had better remember to give Joshua a hug. If I forgot, as I walked away after tucking him under the covers, he'd say, "Mama!" His outstretched arms waited for me.

When I stooped, Joshua wrapped his pudgy arms around my neck and squeezed.

This mama closed her eyes and sank into a sweet-smelling embrace.

I cherished my son, Lord. Thank You for bringing him into our family. I'm grateful. Through Jesus, Amen.

~Your Mother Memories~

~Your Prayer of Praise~

~A Scripture of Encouragement~

FOUR: Saint Patrick's Day before Dawn

Fear not, for I am with you; be not dismayed, for I am your God; I will strengthen you, I will help you, I will uphold you with my righteous right hand.

—Isaiah 41:10

I woke long before dawn the next morning from a night of fitful dozing. Saint Patrick's Day had been a time to consider our Irish heritage, but Joshua's soldier heart left the war of life on Earth.

Within minutes of waking, the phone rang at my bedside table. Candy Arlington, the coauthor of the suicide survivor book *Aftershock*, was on the other line. She identified herself as a friend of a friend. I said, "Please, pray for us now."

She recited the *Lord's Prayer* loud enough for both of us to hear. How comforting the moment. God's mercies delivered in the form of Candy, to meet us, Joshua's parents, in our loneliest, most wretched hour.

After the prayer, Candy spoke reassuring words and ended the call by saying she would mail her book to me.

Later, I found hope within its pages. As I read *Aftershock*, it became clear countless mothers had been losing children since the beginning. Eve lost her son, Abel, and I lost my son, Joshua.

Father, You sent Candy. A divine appointment. You use Your saints to show how much You care and to prove You will never leave or forsake us. In Christ, Amen.

A Mother's Memories

Within two weeks of bringing him home from the hospital as an infant, Joshua caught a cold.

More colds and ear infections followed throughout his first winter. The side effects of the antibiotics tore at his stomach.

When Joshua was four months old, we moved out of the house for two days and a night. We had the house sprayed for fleas, believing these insects caused the red blisters on his body.

The next morning he woke with a fever, covered in dime-sized welts. How could blisters change to welts when we're not at home?

Grabbing Joshua's bottle of liquid antibiotics, I said, "What's in this?" I read the label and found cherry flavoring as an ingredient. "We're taking Joshua to the hospital."

The doctor ordered a test. Results showed Joshua's blood had an infection, most likely caused by the cherry flavoring. He prescribed a mint-flavor in Joshua's antibiotic, warning us to allow no other.

I sighed in relief and took my baby home.

Father, thank You for hearing my prayer to help little Joshua. In the name of Jesus, Amen.

~Your Mother Memories~

~Your Prayer of Praise~

~A Scripture of Encouragement~

FIVE: Upon Rising

He who dwells in the shelter of the Most High will abide in the shadow of the Almighty.

—Psalm 91:1

We arose from bed the first morning after Joshua's suicide, anticipating our eldest son Jason's arrival from a distance of five hundred miles.

We found out later he stopped in the night to sleep for three hours, and then drove the rest of the way to our home.

At six a.m., we opened the door to his knock, less than twenty-four hours after Joshua had died. Jason's mouth was turned down, his blue eyes dulled in disbelief.

I collapsed into *his* arms in childlike abandonment. Later, I hugged Jason's three children, hung on a bit too long, and kissed their faces.

My daughter-in-law carried a baby within her womb at six months in gestation. My unborn grandchild moved the moment we two women embraced. *Thump.* The baby smacked my stomach.

I drew back in surprise. "This baby kicked me hard." At this moment, I thanked God for the life growing inside the warm and safe place she called home.

Even in our fresh grief, Lord, You give me hope by way of a thump from an unborn baby. Through Christ, I thank You, Amen.

A Mother's Memories

I have stored in the memories of my heart two sons napping on the bed.

Jason would fall asleep with Joshua, after singing a Jesus song to his baby brother. I'd take a snapshot of the two in a snuggled position.

One photograph is of Jason and Joshua cupped together on their sides. With Joshua facing his brother's back, his leg was slung over Jason.

At those perfect snapped moments, my eyes glistened for the joy of being their mother.

Father, You've blessed me with two sons. Because of Jesus, I'm glad, Amen.

~Your Mother Memories~

~Your Prayer of Praise~

~A Scripture of Encouragement~

SIX: Saint Patrick's Day Mid-Morning

They will console you, when you see their ways and their deeds, and you shall know that I have not done without cause all that I have done in it, declares the Lord GOD.

—Ezekiel 14:23

Jason hung the Irish flag in honor of his brother.

Soon after, friends came to comfort. My pain was too great to bear alone, so to anyone who asked I unburdened our horror.

Growing tired quickly, though, my mind dulled, unable to accept the reality of Joshua's death.

I never would have imagined how God could bring joy into the day. The noise of it flowed in the squeals and laughter of our seven grandchildren.

Unintended, I smiled at them, but then sorrow overwhelmed my soul once again. Uncle Joshy would not see them grow up, nor ever meet the new baby.

Will the older children forget their uncle Joshy?

My thoughts were interrupted when someone told me visitors waited outside our front door.

My gentle friend Mona and her husband stood on our porch. They held love in their hands: sheet music they wanted to perform for Joshua's memorial.

I chose "Danny Boy" and allowed them to decide on the hymns. And in our circle, we cupped palms together. Whispered prayers fell from their lips, flowing from their hearts to claim them as mine.

Tears dried for the moment, and I drew strength from their confidence in God. Earth angels in action.

Thank You, Holy Father, for blessing us with folks who do Your work. Through the name of Jesus, Amen.

A Mother's Memories

"Look, Mama!" Three-year-old Joshua held a ratty kitten in the air. "I found him in the dump."

I shook my head. "But, honey, I'm allergic to cats. Where will we keep it?" Looking closer, I gasped. "This thing is filthy. See the fleas crawling?"

Joshua cuddled the creature's matted fur, and a flea hopped on his cheek. "I'll give him a bath, Mama," and off our little guy ran.

Going about my kitchen chores, my heart softened at the image of how Joshua's eyes danced. Shrugging, I said to myself, "A kitten may teach him responsibility."

The animal splashed and meowed in the tub. Minutes later, Joshua brought to me the wet, scrawny cat half-wrapped in a towel with its legs dangling.

"See, Mama, he's all clean."

I peered at Joshua's pet. "We need to feed him milk."

My son's lips curved upward. "Yep, he's hungry."

Lord, even though the kitten was not a blessing to me, You gifted Joshua with a furry friend. I enjoyed seeing my son happy, and I cherish this memory. In Christ, Amen.

~Your Mother Memories~

~Your Prayer of Praise~

~A Scripture of Encouragement~

SEVEN: Saint Patrick's Day Afternoon

For affliction does not come from the dust, nor does trouble sprout from the ground.

—Job 5:6

Joshua's brother, sister, daddy, and I made the short trip into town to choose a mortuary for his cremation.

The first place? Too formal.

Across the street, though, we spotted two Irish names on a sign. Another mortuary business. With this one glance, I nodded.

When we told the mortician our son had died by his own hand, he tucked his chin to his chest as though in prayer.

Several long moments passed. He lifted his eyes now filled with moisture.

"This is a sad, sad day."

In soft tones, the mortician asked us questions. He made a phone call to have Joshua's body sent to his place of business, and my children and I examined urns in a display case a few steps away.

After the three of us agreed upon an urn we believed Joshua would appreciate, Jami and Jason sat in two chairs along the wall.

I returned to where I had sat at the desk. My adult children once again looked like the wide-eyed six- and seven-year-olds they'd been when I was in labor with their baby brother.

My eyes blurred. I grieved for their suffering.

What happened to our family? Our baby boy? Their witty brother? The adult son?

Just then the mortician held his hand over the phone mouthpiece and stared at us.

He explained, "The coroner cannot find powder burns on your son's fingers."

My stomach lurched. With horror climbing up my throat, I was about to lose my meager breakfast.

Father, please don't allow this to worsen. Expose the truth. We cannot bear any more. In the holiness of Jesus, I beg, Amen.

A Mother's Memories

Before Joshua's birth, I had chosen four boy names.

In the hospital, Joshua came to us in the five o'clock evening hour. We spent the night, and the next day we chose his name.

I asked Jami and Jason to decide from my choices because I wanted to call him Jeremiah Joshua Jacob Williams.

Discussing it among each other, they both said, "We like Joshua."

We'd call him Josh. It sounded strong like the way his neck muscles held his head hours after being born.

We also decided Joshua didn't need a middle name, like the Biblical leader who took over for Moses.

Signing the papers, we made it legal and took our baby home.

Lord, You have blessed me. You have given me a family of five. Thank You, Father. In Jesus, I'm elated, Amen

~Your Mother Memories~

~Your Prayer of Praise~

~A Scripture of Encouragement~

EIGHT: Day Two

God will send out his steadfast love and his faithfulness!
—Psalm 57:3

After the previous day mortician visit, the phone rang early the next morning. "Mrs. Williams?"

I trembled, recognizing the gentleman's voice. "Yes?"

"They found the powder burns."

Relieved, I swallowed a sob. I could not have imagined going through an investigation.

We knew the truth.

Thank the Lord further inspection with a keener eye proved it.

Now, the mortician said, "To view Joshua's body today, please be here at one o'clock."

I gulped back tears of a different sort. *Oh. Joshua's body. My last goodbye.*

We prepared to leave for the mortuary while our children's spouses and our grandchildren made two banners for the memorial.

One project lay across the dining room table as busy hands created. The other project draped along the picnic table on the patio.

Before I shut the front door, one of our grandchildren squealed with delight. I imagined it was her turn to place a hand into colored paint and press her print onto the banner for her uncle Joshy.

As I climbed into the front seat of the car, I reflected on this hand-print banner the children were making. The felt letters glued on read, "We love and miss you, Uncle Joshy."

Dear loving Father, I am grateful for Your protection and answered prayer. Please get us through the next step. Through Christ, I ask, Amen.

A Mother's Memories

When we moved to Oklahoma, the biggest concern was not the rainstorms, tornadoes, or insects that were three times the normal size on the west coast.

One day after a heavy rain, water rose around our brick house. Jason rode his bicycle in the flood. Joshua zoomed on a Big Wheel with water up to his seat.

It was warm out, so I wasn't concerned about him becoming sick. From the open front door, I smiled at the playground the weather had created for my boys.

Jason waved at me, riding in circles around Joshua. "Boy, Mom, it doesn't rain like this in California."

Much later, Jason hollered from the back door, "We need two jars with lids, Mom."

Coming to meet them, I gasped. The boys were a muddy disaster, but then they were having fun. "Why do you need jars?"

Joshua grinned, his eyes dancing. "We found really big worms, Mama."

I placed two Mason jars on the porch steps. Jason lifted the extra-large, black worms between two sticks and dropped them into a jar. He took the sticks and trapped one of the worms and placed it in the other jar.

Jason screwed on both lids. "I'm taking mine to school for show-and-tell."

The next afternoon about the time when school let out, the phone rang.

"Mrs. Williams?"

"Yes."

"This is Jason's teacher, Mrs. Gray."

I smiled. "Oh, hi."

"Um, Mrs. Williams. Are you, uh, aware of what your son brought to school today?"

"Of course. A large worm." There was silence on the other end of the phone line.

"Is something wrong, Mrs. Gray? Was it not show-and-tell today?"

"Uh, yes. But, this is no worm. It's a snake—a water moccasin, Mrs. Williams. One bite is capable of killing a grown man before you can get him to the hospital. Not only that, but the babies, like the one your son brought, are even more poisonous."

Gulp. We had no hospital in our town.

My thoughts raced to Joshua's worm in the jar on his chest of drawers. I shivered.

"I'm sorry, Mrs. Gray. I didn't know. Gotta go!"

Letting go of the phone, it dropped into the cradle. I raced to the boys' bedroom.

As Joshua napped, I reached for the jar and wrapped it, snake and all, in several grocery bags. My hands shaking, I pushed it deep into the outside trash.

Lord, when Joshua rode his Big Wheel in the water of snakes, Your angels protected him and his big brother. In the name of Jesus, I thank You, Lord God, Amen.

34

~Your Mother Memories~

~Your Prayer of Praise~

~A Scripture of Encouragement~

NINE: Afternoon on Day Two

Behold, he taketh away, who can hinder him? Who will say unto him, What doest thou?

—Job 9:12 KJV

A relative followed us to the mortuary, where we would view Joshua's body.

As we walked through the opened double doors, I cupped between my hands a tiny bottle of anointing oil. The receptionist showed us to the room where Joshua's body lay.

Jami and Jason hung back.

Walking ahead of everyone, I came to a stop and stroked my son's now-cold hands and pale face. "Hi, Son," I whispered. "I love you. I already miss you." Someone in the background heaved with sobs. "I'm going to anoint your body for burial, baby."

Unscrewing the cap, my work began. I tipped the opened bottle onto my fingers, then caressed Joshua's forehead. Saying goodbye with each drop of the oil, the Holy Spirit's peace swaddled this mama.

After a few minutes, I sensed my other children behind me close enough to touch. "Do you want to help?"

Jami stood beside me wringing her hands. I offered her some of the oil. Hesitating, she unwound her fingers and opened her palm.

Pouring the oil for her to anoint Joshua in good-bye, I sensed Jason on my other side. His breathing labored with obvious sorrow. He offered the pad of one finger. I tipped the bottle to allow a drop of oil to fall on his skin.

Pulling off Joshua's socks, I rubbed oil on his feet with the two crooked toes—toes just like his mama's.

Someone said, "It's time to go, Jean."

"But there's more oil." The torment in my loved one's eyes—.

"Okay, then."

We drifted toward the door, but a part of me had been left with the oil on Joshua's skin. I slowed.

Glancing over a shoulder, my soul grew thirsty for one last glimpse.

"Good-bye, Son," I whispered, kissing two fingers and reaching with them to what was once my Joshua.

Oh, holy, holy One, I cannot bear to leave. Please, may we go back in time? Before the day he died? Give us another chance to change this. Through Your Son, I beg of You, Amen.

A Mother's Memories

I can't count the times I sat with toddler Joshua in the steamed bathroom with orders for no one to open the door.

Croup plagued Joshua's early years, and some days we lived in the steamy atmosphere. I'd hold him on my lap and show him how to take deep breaths, exaggerating to make a game of it.

When Joshua learned to say a few words and felt croupy, he told me, "Mama, I need steam." In we would go to our sanctuary.

Yet, it amazed me how resilient was my little son. One time his nose ran in a constant stream. To avoid wiping his reddened and cracked skin, we stuck tissue in his nostrils.

He chased his brother and sister through the house growling. Of course, his siblings played along and acted scared, for which Joshua amped up the monster noises.

My rich mother's milk sustained him in the first years, although I received worried looks and advice from people when they discovered Joshua's solid-food strikes. But from the day of his birth, Joshua never lost an ounce of fat.

His pediatrician even commented once, "As sick as this baby gets, you'd never know it by how he keeps gaining."

Yes, Joshua thrived as a chubby baby until long after he found his legs and ran.

I felt sorry Joshua was such a sick child, yet the worst was still to come. As he grew, he suffered through strep throat, mononucleosis, and finally crippling arthritis. I hoped and prayed Joshua would outgrow being ill.

I'm grateful, Lord, for my milk which kept Joshua fed and satisfied. Nursing him was a bright spot in an otherwise difficult time for both of us. Through Jesus's blessed name, I praise You, Amen.

~Your Mother Memories~

~Your Prayer of Praise~

~A Scripture of Encouragement~

TEN: Third Day

Blessed be God, even the Father of our Lord Jesus Christ, the Father of mercies, and God of all comfort.

—2 Corinthians 1:3 KJV

I dressed in black—a rayon dress with a narrow red trim. White pearls hung loose about my neck—a gift from my husband for my fiftieth birthday months earlier.

Our cousins and their children arrived at the house and got to work cleaning the living room and kitchen. My aunt hugged me. Sinking into her soft chest, I wept.

Too soon, it was time to leave.

Slipping into Joshua's forest-green suede coat, my cheek nestled against the jacket collar. Eyes closed, I inhaled Joshua's scent.

Lord, why is he not here to wear this?

As we drove to the memorial service, I glanced toward the backseat at Joshua's gray-speckled urn. The urn our children and I had chosen.

My fingers had fastened it snug in the middle seat belt, as though Joshua were a child again sitting between his siblings.

A lightning bolt stab ripped within my heart area, and I stifled a sob. Oh, Lord God, this can't be happening. Not to us. Facing the front, tears streamed along my cheeks in silent cries.

Pulling into the church building parking lot, mourners overflowed outside the double doors. Some of the folks I'd never met before.

A friend handed each person a twig of mistletoe when they entered the building. As a youngster, Joshua used to stand under the kissing greenery and wait for me to see him. He'd do the same for his grandmother Williams.

40

I was glad we designated someone to hand out the mistletoe.

The service opened with "Amazing Grace" by a bagpipe player. Joshua would have loved the pipes, and especially the gentleman's Scottish attire.

A wail escaped from my lips at the significance of this moment. A family member draped an arm around my shoulder and gave me a protective squeeze.

Mercifully, our preacher spoke about how wrong it was to believe a person who died by suicide meant an automatic sentence to hell and not a final destiny in heaven.

My friend Mona and her husband played and sang "Danny Boy." God bless Mona, for at one point she drew in a deep breath to stifle her own sob, and continued singing.

Joshua's brother and sister and two friends spoke a few words. His dearest buddy, Dana McGregor, read a Scripture.

One of Joshua's friends was assigned to pass out candles and have someone help to light them.

When I nodded for him to begin, his eyes filled with tears, and he bowed his head.

So I gave people the candles and lit them. Everyone sang a hymn to close the service.

Greeting folks afterward, I thanked them as they filed through the open double door. I was awed by the turnout of more than two hundred fifty acquaintances, friends, and family members.

We are not alone. We walk this path with the Lord and Jesus, and with our loved ones. Thank You, Father. Through Your Son, I come before You, Amen.

41

A Mother's Memories

"Mama, I'm going to be the Hulk, like on TV, when I grow up."

Joshua made this announcement when he turned three. At thirteen he created a weight training program to fit his goals and showed commitment.

His new dream was to make it into the Navy SEALs.

For two years, he read everything available on this career choice. He ate healthy and drank the body-builder formulas.

Joshua, the driven one.

Before his fifteenth birthday, Joshua's feet, hands, and elbows became red and swollen with pain.

His dream died a slow death with the diagnosis: ankylosing spondylitis, a rare form of rheumatoid arthritis.

Joshua took a break from pumping iron, while he and I read several books on how to rebuild his immune system.

After six months of massages, saunas, hot tubs, cold pool swims, and eating organic foods (still no sugars), Joshua's excessive pain eased. He was able to light-weight train.

Facing his reality, Joshua came to me and announced, "Mom, you can't have a health problem in your medical record and get into the SEALs."

His eyes shimmered with unshed tears.

At the time, I didn't understand the full extent of his sorrow until I read the journals he left for us to read.

Lord, this was the first of many heart-wrenching, broken dreams for Joshua. I was sad for my youngest child. In the name of Jesus, I ached for him and prayed, Amen.

~Your Mother Memories~

~Your Prayer of Praise~

~A Scripture of Encouragement~

ELEVEN: Day Four

The Lord is my shepherd; I shall not want.

—Psalm 23:1

The day after Joshua's memorial, my appetite growled.

My food groups up until Joshua's death consisted of dairy, grains, fruits, vegetables, and chicken. Now, I couldn't eat enough steak or salsa.

I thought it odd because I ate little meat before, and I never cared for red meat. Later, I read our bodies crave and need extra protein when we're under tremendous stress. As far as salsa, hot peppers release happy endorphins.

Also, having been a healthy eater for twenty-five years, my conscience stung with guilt for giving in to the cravings of sugared chocolates. And most of my indulgences *were* organic sweets.

But, sometimes nothing satisfied for the moment like the color-coated chocolate candies or the vanilla cream-filled tea cookies with milk.

A hypocrite to my way of thinking, I knew better than to eat the sweet, empty-calorie foods. This created new stress heaped upon my guilt for not having been able to save my son.

Over the months, I understood the need for comfort foods like dairy, although the junk food part was a detriment to my health.

And as I snacked, my soul longed for a closer relationship with the Lord. I asked myself countless times, "Why isn't God enough? Why can't He be enough for me?"

The unhealthy sugar cravings passed in time as fresh, raw grief was replaced with a will to live in the midst of my loss. Although, right after Joshua's service, I could not have imagined how harsh my reality would still become in those first grieving years.

Lord, I appreciate the wholesome comfort foods for which You created for us to enjoy. In the name of Christ, Amen.

A Mother's Memories

When Joshua was one-year-old I met a kind herbalist.

Downtown at a street fair, we slowed in front of her booth. She peered into Joshua's eyes and said, "This baby is sick."

She handed me her card and told me to call her anytime. *How does she know?* In awe by this encounter, I thanked her. My son still hadn't stayed well for more than two weeks at a stretch.

Not knowing anything about natural healing, I hurried on with my children.

A few weeks later, Joshua became sick with bronchitis. His fever rose during the evenings. After sitting with him in the rocking chair for two nights, I remembered the herbalist's card. I looked at the clock: midnight.

It was either take him to the emergency room or call her. I prayed and dialed her number. I told her my name and where we'd met. "I'm sorry it's so late, but my baby has bronchitis with a high fever."

After a short pause in our conversation, the herbalist said, "Do you have any cabbage?"

"Yes."

"This is what you do, Jean." She cleared her throat. "Place several leaves of cabbage on his bare chest. Wrap his chest with plastic wrap, going around several times. Keep him in a warm shirt. It could take eight hours, but this will loosen the mucus. Let me know when it does."

I did as she instructed, all the while, I thought, *Am I stupid to try to heal my baby with a vegetable?*

I kept asking God if this was the right thing. Slipping Joshua into his pajama top, I sensed God's peace. I tucked Joshua in his trundle bed, and I fell asleep next to him.

At eight the next morning, I awoke to Joshua's gagging coughs. I grabbed under his arms and hauled him to the bathroom, where he vomited into the commode. I was stunned at how much mucous my child had expelled.

After bathing Joshua and dressing him into clean pajamas, I thought he'd be exhausted. He had other plans. Joshua wiggled from my arms and toddled into the toy room.

In astonishment, I took his temperature. Normal. I wrinkled my brows. Cabbage leaves healed my baby?

When I called the herbalist and told her, she said, "I'm not surprised. What was interesting to me was you had cabbage in your refrigerator." We both laughed.

From this experience, I used a select few herbs the herbalist suggested for whatever illness Joshua caught. He no longer took the antibiotics which caused his stomach cramps.

As a result he stayed well longer. But, it didn't escape my notice: Joshua had a tendency to become sick more often than the average child.

Thank You, Lord, for creating foods to heal our bodies. In Your Son, I'm grateful, Amen.

~Your Mother Memories~

~Your Prayer of Praise~

~A Scripture of Encouragement~

TWELVE: Day Six

But even the hairs of your head are all numbered.

—Matthew 10:30

On the Monday after Joshua's memorial service, I was scheduled to begin an online editing class or drop out.

I told a few family members how glad I was the class was online and not in a physical school. Their faces took on frowns, or all expressions were erased.

Maybe they wondered how I could do anything normal this soon after Joshua's death.

In my heart, I thanked the Lord God, for it would be a respite from my reality. However, there were hindrances.

The morning I was to begin, I arose before dawn. Later in the day would be too late, as my crying spells hit me and grew worse into the night.

Also, my attention span had shortened to ten minutes in the early grieving days. My head hurt to concentrate for much longer.

I sat at my desk, pushed the "on" button of my computer—and sighed—relieved for some normalcy.

My mind worked hard to bring about a string of coherent thoughts. This jolted me.

Maybe my family's bewildered looks were justified. How could I do something as basic as take a class? Joshua ended his life six days before in the room next door.

With God's help I can do all things, and I finished the class in the designated time allowed.

Father, before I registered for the class, You knew I would need this to keep my mind busy. Thank You, Lord. Through Jesus, I pray, Amen.

A Mother's Memories

Eleven-year-old Joshua ran into the house, slamming the door behind him.

"Mom, Mom, the mean boys are chasing me again."

For the past week, while doing his newspaper route, my son had been harassed by a teenage gang. The tone of his voice told me he'd had enough.

Joshua whipped around the corner of the kitchen, catching me dusting our knickknacks.

"I've got to deliver my papers. What am I gonna do, Mom?"

I cocked my head, holding the dust rag. "Do you want me to go along? I'm sure they won't bother you then."

Joshua lowered his head. "I guess."

I stepped closer to him. "Look at me, Son."

Tears brimmed in his eyes. "Why do those guys have to bother me?"

I patted his arm. "Some people have small-thinking minds. Tomorrow I'll go with you. We'll make it fun."

The next day, Joshua pointed out the cluster of boys who had shouted insults and threatened to steal his bike.

Planting my sneakers on the ground, I stopped my bicycle and jumped off.

Fists on my hips, I glared at each of them. I was prepared to tell them I'd call the police if they didn't leave Joshua alone.

They walked off with glances over their shoulders.

For the next few weeks, Joshua and I rode daily on his paper route. Some of the older customers praised Joshua for being responsible.

Even though Joshua eventually quit the route, I enjoyed our time together. We raced each other on the bikes, chatted about school and his friends, and explored the side trails.

Best of all, Joshua knew his mom was someone he could count on.

Father, those times of being scared were humiliating for Joshua. He worked hard, and I was proud of him. In Christ, Amen.

~Your Mother Memories~

~Your Prayer of Praise~

~A Scripture of Encouragement~

THIRTEEN: Day Seven

Answer me when I call, O God of my righteousness! You have given me relief when I was in distress. Be gracious to me and hear my prayer!

—Psalm 4:1

I sorted through Joshua's personal keepsakes and found yellow, lined paper folded in fourths.

I read the words he had handwritten in bold, black ink:

Dear Mom, I have let everyone down. I had no way of knowing, but I believe because of my low immune system at the time, what was a harmless dose of cough syrup to others became toxic to my system. It affected my brain chemicals somehow. Saying all this now doesn't make anything better. I'm sorry for that. I just want to apologize. I know this can't be easy on you, and I'm sorry for any pain and suffering my foolish actions have caused you and Dad.

Nothing has gone the way I hoped it would. I'm sorry for that. I'm very responsible and very guilty for putting you guys through all this. I know it's all my fault, but I can't do anything about it. Life is anything but fair. I always thought by this time I would be graduating college and as normal as can be. Who knew? It's such a strange world for things to be able to change so quickly. I just want to apologize for everything.

I bowed my head.

Pressed the letter to my chest.

Fought to breathe.

Oh, Father, Holy One, as my son wrote this note, You knew one day I would find it and weep. Please forgive me for not understanding better what Joshua was going through. I failed my son. I regret he didn't understand we needed him as he was, poor health, poor mind at the end, and all. In Jesus's holy name, I pray, for I'm devastated, Amen.

A Mother's Memories

"Mrs. Williams, it's just not allowed to have a kindergartener on the wrestling team."

Hoping to change his mind, I said, "Well, Coach, let Joshua wrestle for the fun of it. You can do this, right?"

The coach stroked his chin. "I could get into trouble, but we'll let Joshua give it a try."

We told Joshua the news, and he hopped on his toes. "I get to wrestle like Jason?"

"Yes, Son," I said.

After several wrestling meets, the coach grinned with his announcement to us.

"Joshua shows great potential. So far, he's won almost every match."

As proud as we were for Joshua, we were also surprised at his aggressive techniques on the wrestling mat.

Eventually, Joshua's drive to win placed him in the Oregon Regional's. This meant if he did well there, he could go on to wrestle at the state level.

After the announcement came over the intercom stating Joshua won regional's, the coach walked off the gym floor to meet us in the bleachers.

"Guys, we have a problem. Joshua is not supposed to be wrestling, and I know State won't accept him. This is the end of wrestling for your son until he's in first grade."

After much thought, we devised a plan to help Joshua accept this decision.

I told him, "Son, you can't wrestle and play Tee ball at the same time. Wouldn't you rather play ball now?"

"Yeah, Mama, I wanna play with my friends." Joshua's smile lit my heart.

Father, thank You for giving us the time of traveling to other schools and watching our boys wrestle. We grew closer as a family. And the memories grow sweeter in my heart. In the name of Christ, Amen.

~Your Mother Memories~

~Your Prayer of Praise~

~A Scripture of Encouragement~

FOURTEEN: Day Eight

"Therefore do not be anxious about tomorrow, for tomorrow will be anxious for itself. Sufficient for the day is its own trouble."
—Matthew 6:34

Too soon our son, Jason, and his family packed their suitcases and prepared to say good-bye.

We agreed Jason should drive Joshua's car back to his home and give it to a large family who needed an extra vehicle.

Watching Joshua's car leaving? I can't express how much this tore at my heart. Even if it was for the best.

But I had no idea what it meant to my fragile emotions.

At this moment, reality smacked me like a fist. For better or worse, we had to get through each day without our Joshua, and now even the largest item he owned.

Never again would I see his red Pontiac parked in our driveway.

Without Joshua, how could I live this life? Unable to wrap my mind around such an absurd idea, I decided to *be* in the moment as much as possible.

I prayed for the Lord to help me achieve this goal: one moment, one hour, and one day at a time.

After Jason and his family left, I tackled spring cleaning.

As I took down our bedroom blinds and washed them in our front yard, two friends pulled their vehicle alongside the curb. They visited for an hour.

During their time at our home, God made it clear. He had not forgotten us. Mercy came after family left and company arrived.

Dear Father, Your loving arms continue to embrace us in our sorrow. Through Jesus, I'm grateful, Amen.

A Mother's Memories

"I'm outta here." Joshua raised his always soft voice to an annoyed holler. Face scrunched in fury, he threw his clothes into a duffle bag.

At eighteen, he had become upset with me and left home.

Three days I sobbed. For one thing, I couldn't imagine any of my children being this furious with me. For another, it was over something trivial.

The summer after Joshua graduated high school, he became difficult to wake in the mornings for his construction job. He had an alarm, but he would shut it off and fall back to sleep.

For about a month, I shook his shoulder and told him, "Son, you're going to be late for work."

At first he got up to the sound of my voice. In time, nothing worked but to throw back his blankets and demand he get out of bed. Now.

I did this one time too many.

Joshua moved in with friends.

The first weekend after Joshua left, our community celebrated the harvest of strawberries with the yearly Strawberry Festival.

My daughter Jami asked me to join her and her two daughters: a baby and a toddler. I never knew when sobs would overtake me, so I declined the invitation.

At the end of two weeks, Joshua moved home as suddenly as he'd left. While he was unpacking his duffle bag, I entered his room.

I clasped my hands together. "Son, I won't bug you anymore about being late for work."

Joshua stared at me with a wide-eyed expression. "Mom, I'm sorry. I wasn't mad at you. I just took stuff bothering me out on you and used it as an excuse."

We hugged each other, and my shoulders heaved with relief.

He patted my head, and in his familiar, gentle voice said, "Don't cry, Little Mama. It wasn't your fault."

Lord, now I understand my son felt safe enough to direct misguided anger toward me. I would never stop loving him. Through Your Son, I'm glad he came home, Amen.

~Your Mother Memories~

~Your Prayer of Praise~

~A Scripture of Encouragement~

FIFTEEN: End of March

Save me, O God; for the waters are come in unto my soul.
— Psalm 69:1 KJV

One afternoon, I wandered the house feeling adrift, as if any moment my skin would crawl off of me.

My mind did an unusual thing which continued sporadically for months. It skipped like a blackout in between thoughts.

God had to hold me, for my whole being was about to split into shards.

I did not understand until months later, I had stuffed some of my grief. This was probably because it had become an automatic response to keep my feelings somewhat in check around family members.

So when a lawn mower roared to life in our neighborhood, I fell to the floor, screaming. No one would hear me having a fit.

I begged God to numb my pain, as I kicked and flailed about on the carpet until exhausted.

I rose. Washed my face. Brushed my disheveled hair.

I could do anything with God by my side.

Still, a shadow hovered, and my grief intensified.

During my early grieving, I realized another problem. I couldn't feel the Lord's love as before. This frightened me.

Finally I recognized a pattern. God's love came through the actions of others.

Lord, do You hear me through my weeping? Can we still have a relationship when all I do is mourn and cry? Help me, oh, Lord, I beg, through Jesus's name, Amen.

A Mother's Memories

When Joshua turned a year old, I sometimes left him and his siblings with a sitter on bi-monthly grocery shopping and errand days. No bending over a car seat to unbuckle Joshua, and haul three children down the aisles.

Each time I backed out of the driveway, Joshua stood on a dining room chair at the window, crying.

At the market I enjoyed my break from housework and three active little people. But half-way through my errands, I imagined Joshua's scrunched, tear-stained cheeks.

Returning home, Joshua's head popped into view at the same window, even before I could open my car door. As I entered the house, Joshua met me in the hallway. He tugged on my skirt and said, "My mama."

I sat on the couch and nursed Joshua, while the rest of the family brought in the groceries and put them away. Kissing his head, I crooned soothing words.

After Joshua finished his milk, he crawled off my lap. Now he toddled over to inspect the grocery bags left on the kitchen floor.

Lord, how blessed You have made me. I needed my time away, but was ready to return to mothering. In Jesus, I praise You, Amen.

~Your Mother Memories~

~Your Prayer of Praise~

~A Scripture of Encouragement~

SIXTEEN: The Month of April

For everything there is a season, and a time for every matter under heaven.

—Ecclesiastes 3:1

After Joshua died, the loss created a pain around my heart which escalated.

Tormented from the ache and lack of sleep, my identity as a mother shredded. However, my love for Joshua intensified, though no love flowed in return from son to mother.

Because of this pain of losing Joshua, I began a nightly ritual. "Please, God, stop my heart's beating."

At first, in the quiet of the house, I listened to music. But, the tunes reminded me of Joshua, either his favorites or songs he didn't care for. Instead of music, I talked out loud, with my son's dog and cat as an occasional audience.

Days alone stretched into weeks, and there was some reprieve as I worked on my current children's novel.

Another outlet to express myself came from my online writers' group. I could email them my woes and this left me encouraged. They even talked to me on the phone, never avoiding my need to share my deepest sorrow.

In the afternoon, though, my crying jags started over again.

During the adjustment time of being alone in the house, I was still tortured by remembering Joshua's fall to the bed and holding him in my arms as his heart stopped.

Would the act of Joshua dying never quit torturing me?

Daily, I wavered between my skin prickling as I passed his closed bedroom door to walking inside and searching through Joshua's possessions. Would I find another clue as to why he died by suicide?

Another note?

Sometimes my grief increased to a height where I forgot the people who would have listened and brought comfort.

Too deep in the pit, it was God and me—alone.

My Lord, my God! The one I want I cannot have, so I want nothing except to sleep. Please be merciful to me through the valley of this shadow. I long to see my son. Through the name of Christ, Amen.

A Mother's Memories

Joshua pushed away his family before he left us.

During his last few years, Joshua grew miserable, emotionally and physically. His face was like a mask void of emotions.

My son's poor health came to the point where he used a cane more often. Bones in his back were fusing together.

The idea Joshua could die by suicide never entered my mind, so I had many regrets over his death. And so when I remembered how we tried to comfort our son, I focused on this as much as possible.

For example, I was glad my husband and I had made the extra effort to keep our home stress-free for Joshua.

I wondered, though, if I should have stepped back and noticed my son through fresh eyes?

One month before Joshua died, he walked outside to where I was hosing off the driveway. "Mom?"

My heart leaped. He hadn't spoken my name in a long while. His solemn face destroyed my moment of joy. I pushed aside my concerns and became grateful for a conversation with my silent and moody child.

"Yes, Son?"

"It's almost spring, isn't it?"

What an odd question. Before I could speak, he said, "I saw a robin yesterday."

Joshua walked back into the house, where I was sure he shut himself into his room.

At the time, I didn't realize what was behind his question.

Since Joshua's death, we've learned the highest suicide rates occur in spring. Not Christmas, as people are led to believe.

The reason given?

The sunny days and the birds singing do not fit the suicidal person's mood. They can't imagine living another day where the earth is breaking out in song and sun.

Father, I'm grateful You allowed us to keep Joshua for as long as we had him. He was almost never born. We would have never known him. In Jesus's holiness, Amen.

~Your Mother Memories~

~Your Prayer of Praise~

~A Scripture of Encouragement~

SEVENTEEN: Easter Sunday

For the LORD your God is a merciful God. He will not leave you.
—Deuteronomy 4:31

Less than a month later, I didn't want to consider Easter.

After church services on this special day, I crawled onto my bed, hoping for sleep. I'd forget the first celebration after Joshua's death.

But our extended family expected us at the home of a relative, and my heart couldn't imagine visiting.

As I lay on the bed, sobs strained my nerves further as I remembered.

At age fifteen, Joshua became a Christian on Easter.

Within an hour later, though, I was on my way to my in-laws.

Tears gushed like rain along my cheeks the entire half-hour trip.

When I walked into the house, I was still crying.

The living room was filled to capacity with women, and their eyes were on me.

What on earth am I doing? I'm making this awkward.

Yet as embarrassed as I was by my weeping, I was unable to stop.

Soon, a niece, Candice, who was a little older than Joshua, sat at my feet and kept her hand on my knee. She stared up at me with such compassion, eyes filled with her tears.

Witnessing her sorrow, I knew for sure me being there was spoiling their Easter. I felt sorry, causing Joshua's cousin to cry. *I shouldn't be here.*

Candice's mom bent over my chair and whispered, "Whatever you want, we'll do it. If you want to go for a ride, we'll go for a ride. If you want to sit here, we'll sit here."

She wrapped her arms around me and quivered.

With her comforting words, my tears stopped. I heaved a sigh and she let me go.

The other women in the room took turns embracing me and giving words of encouragement.

Mercy came this hour in the form of ladies whom I love.

Lord, You propelled me into the year of firsts without my son, and showed me a community I could trust. They needed to grieve with me. Through Jesus, I praise You, Amen.

A Mother's Memories

Fifteen-year-old Joshua walked into the laundry room. "Mom, I need to be baptized."

I swung round to face him, my arms full of unfolded clothes.

"Really, Son? Do you want Preacher Van Wormer to baptize you?"

He nodded. "Yep, this is what I want."

I dropped my clothes in the clean basket. "Do you understand why you need baptism?"

"Yeah. Our Bible teacher's been teaching us about the importance of baptism."

Stepping closer, I hugged my son. "I'm so glad for this day, Joshua. You are indeed grown-up."

He grinned and leaned against the dryer. "Would you call the preacher for me?"

"Sure. When do you want to do this?"

Joshua pressed his lips together in thought. "How about I be baptized on Easter Sunday? It's only a couple of days away."

I called the preacher, and it became a date.

Joshua had become a quiet teen, and I wasn't certain how he was handling the diagnosis of rheumatoid arthritis.

He would need God's courage and comfort as ankylosing spondylitis took his physical strength.

Just as planned, Joshua became a Christian on Easter Day. This marked one of the happiest moments for our youngest child and us his family.

Thank You, Lord, for bringing my baby to Your Son, Jesus Christ. Through His holy name, I'm grateful, Amen.

~Your Mother Memories~

~Your Prayer of Praise~

~A Scripture of Encouragement~

EIGHTEEN: A Daughter's Love

It is of the Lord's mercies that we are not consumed, because his compassions fail not.

—Lamentations 3:22 KJV

The day came for our granddaughter, Carley's, sixth birthday, and Jami held the party at her house.

I couldn't grasp this celebration without Joshua, so I would learn how in this grieving process.

We arrived, but our tears made us late, and we entered the large crowd of people from both sides of the family.

The solemn faces of those whom we hadn't seen since the memorial made me feel sad for them.

I hoped to make it easy on them and didn't mention the void in our lives.

Nor did I bring up Joshua's name to reassure myself no one would forget he once walked among us.

In a quiet spot of her house, my daughter and I cried together. We only needed each other for this moment—a cleansing release.

Jami wanted to talk about Joshua. She'd had a special bonding with her baby brother, taking her job seriously from the beginning as his second mama.

In our early grieving stage, Jami expressed how she felt about her loss of Joshua. This helped me.

Weeping freely, we soaked each other's shoulders. We smiled sad smiles at the messes on our shirts—evidence from tears and runny noses for someone no longer here.

Father, I could have not have managed without my daughter. Thank You for giving Jami to me. Her strong spirit gave me courage. In Jesus, Amen.

A Mother's Memories

Any time I needed to get my housework done, baby Joshua decided I should hold him instead.

He loved to straddle my hip while I vacuumed, so I accomplished at least one job. But cleaning the bathroom, sweeping, or scrubbing the floor on hands and knees was not possible.

Jami, at eight years old, was more than willing to take Joshua for a wagon ride on the sidewalk in front of our house so I could work.

I'd prop Joshua in with blankets, he'd hold on to the sides of the wagon, and off they'd go.

The first time Jami took him, Joshua craned his neck with a puzzled expression to keep track of me. I waved good-bye.

Jami, the ever-so-smart girl, distracted with an animated voice, "Oh, looky over here, Joshua. See the birds?" He broke his stare and turned from me to see the excitement.

At other times when she played with Joshua, Jami told him, "You're my baby, too."

She loved to play teacher with Joshua. He was her little student; she taught him to talk and pronounce his words correctly.

Right before he was one-year-old, our family understood his simple phrases.

For example, Joshua would point at food on the grocery shelf. "I want some, Jami—yum, yum."

We took for granted Joshua's ability to talk as an older baby.

This was not so for strangers.

One day, when Joshua told one of us he wanted something in the grocery aisle, a lady gasped as she passed us.

She said to her companion, "Did you hear that baby? He just talked."

With a big sister who spent time with her baby brother, Joshua couldn't help but be advanced for his age.

And, he knew how much he was loved.

Thank You again, Father, for giving me a daughter with a loving and willing heart. Jami has blessed me. She is a gift from heaven. In the name of Christ, Amen.

~Your Mother Memories~

~Your Prayer of Praise~

~A Scripture of Encouragement~

NINETEEN: What Left Me Empty, What Filled My Cup

For I consider that the sufferings of this present time are not worth comparing with the glory that is to be revealed to us.

—Romans 8:18

Worn to a frazzle over the loss of Joshua, the worst crying spells came after sunset.

I learned to get most of my night time chores completed early. And the first time I sat down to watch a crime program on TV, it overwhelmed me.

I couldn't sit there and watch death. Nor could I watch family sitcoms as though life was normal. Joshua's gone. He won't be coming back. Never one to enjoy this type of viewing, I switched off the set.

I needed wholesome laughter to relieve some of the grief which built over the day, so we watched classic comedies like Lucille Ball and Red Skelton.

Oftentimes, I retired early to read in the quiet of my room. I studied the Bible, a concordance within reach to dissect the Scriptures for clarification.

The questions of most importance: where was Joshua's soul and what did the Bible say about heaven and hell?

More than ever before, God's Word became my lifeline, my hope.

For simple pleasure, I read stacks of middle-grade children's books, which included rereads of the *Little House on the Prairie* series.

It had been just a few short months since Joshua's death. I worked hard to remember to depend on the Lord and watch for His blessings. Otherwise, I would drown in a chasm of grief.

Father, please guide me in my choice of books to read and movies to watch. I'm grateful for wholesome comedy, allowing me to rest my mind for a moment. Through Christ's abundant love, Amen.

A Mother's Memories

"Where is Carissa Plains, Son?"

Joshua scratched at his ear. "Not sure, but I'll find out. I've been told there are antelopes and flat land with no trees. It'll take several hours for us to drive through."

"I don't know, Joshua." I dried my hands on a kitchen towel. "Sounds desolate."

"That's what I like about it, Mom. Come on, it'll be fun."

My twenty-three-year-old son had taken a liking to road trips. I enjoyed them also, but this one sounded remote.

Should we traipse off into the wild yonder and beyond?

After much thought, I decided it was a fantastic idea for Joshua to get away and forget about his problems.

The next week, we were sightseeing on Carissa Plains.

We stopped frequently to scope the area with our binoculars in search of antelopes.

We were rewarded halfway into our trip. Joshua pointed. "I see one, there."

He handed me the binos. Sure enough, one lone antelope stared at us from a distance of about a quarter of a mile.

I gave Joshua the binoculars for another turn and he his mouth opened and his lips lifted.

My mother's heart warmed to see my son enjoying nature.

God, what Joshua and I shared on the plains was another bonding moment. I sensed our adult friendship, more than just mother and son. Through the comfort of Jesus, Amen.

~Your Mother Memories~

~Your Prayer of Praise~

~A Scripture of Encouragement~

TWENTY: Grieving Animals

O give thanks unto the LORD; for he is good: for his mercy endureth forever.

—Psalm 118:29 KJV

When I began the process of packing Joshua's room, an odd thing occurred.

His cat, LiahNora, a contented outside kitty, jumped on Joshua's window ledge and howled.

After the third such incident in so many days, I straightened from where I was bent over a box and studied at LiahNora.

Tears stung my eyes.

"Poor kitty misses her Joshua."

What about Joshua's Rottweiler, Heinrich? I walked to the backyard where the dog stayed.

I kept him fed and provided fresh water, but otherwise ignored the poor animal.

Considering him now, Heinrich no longer wolfed down his food in mere minutes, often letting the meal sit. On closer inspection his eyes were also droopy.

Sitting at the picnic table bench, I patted my thigh. "Come, boy."

He approached me and I guided his head to my lap and rubbed my fingers through his fur.

I no longer had Joshua to care for, but his animals needed my love and attention.

Lord, You made animals with feelings, and until now, I never knew they could grieve. I'm grateful to have Joshua's pets as my companions and a connection to my son. Looking to the blessings through Jesus, Amen.

A Mother's Memories

Two weeks before Joshua died he stood on the front porch, near where I was pulling weeds in my flowerbed below. "Mom?"

I stopped my work. "Yes, Son?"

He kept his head bowed, eyes averted, as was his habit those last few years. "I'm giving you LiahNora."

Sitting back on my heels, I said, "Why would you do this?"

He stared at the ground. "I'm tired of taking care of her."

Being more of a dog person, I chuckled. "This means I can give her away?"

Joshua jerked his head round to face me, and his frown grew fierce. His voice raised a notch higher. "You can't."

I stood and reached to touch his arm, but he took a step back. I softened my tone. "Son, I'm just teasing."

He stared at me. "You can have Heinrich, too."

He went back into the house before I could form any words.

A bad taste crawled to the top of my throat.

I pondered this turn of events until after Joshua's death, when it became terribly clear.

Father in heaven, I didn't understand my son. Please forgive me for not helping him better. In the name of Jesus, I ask, Amen.

~Your Mother Memories~

~Your Prayer of Praise~

~A Scripture of Encouragement~

TWENTY-ONE: A Mother like Me

The sacrifices of God are a broken spirit: a broken and a contrite heart. Oh, God, thou wilt not despise.

—Psalm 51:17 KJV

A friend told me about a woman named Margaret who had lost a young child.

I stared at Margaret's phone number but wasn't yet ready to call. Weeks later, I gathered my courage and dialed her number.

Kind and easy to talk with, Margaret shared about her own loss and told me about *The Compassionate Friends* organization.

Margaret gave me the number of the woman who printed and mailed *The Compassionate Friends'* regional newsletter.

This lady had lost a son to suicide, also. Margaret assured me the lady would help me in my journey of loss and understanding.

Setting the phone onto its cradle, I sensed a hope. Within *The Compassionate Friends*, there were other parents like us?

Yes, even those who suffer the sorrow of losing a child to suicide.

Oh, my dear Lord. You have shown me I am not alone in my grieving. You bring about blessing from loss. I thank You through Your Son, Amen.

A Mother's Memory

When Joshua was three years old, our family took a vacation, and we stopped in the state of Colorado.

Driving over one bridge, we poked our heads through open car windows to look hundreds of feet down. We craned our necks at the rocks which peaked like pinnacles against the sky.

As it was getting late in the afternoon, we drove to the top of one such bluff to camp for the night.

Everyone piled out of the car, and we stood in awe. Land spread before us for miles. Our children clustered together, pointing and exclaiming about how high we were over the world.

Suddenly, Joshua broke away from our family group and ran toward the edge. With swift legs running, Jason grabbed Joshua before he reached the deep chasm.

Jason's keen sense to notice details showed him there were no protective railings. I thought there were.

Coming from a state which fenced dangerous sightseeing areas, we were shaken to tears to find nothing but air where Joshua was headed.

Surely Joshua's guardian angel nudged Jason into action, and he saved his little brother's life.

Oh, Lord, I'm grateful we were able to keep Joshua for twenty-two more years. In Jesus's blessed name, Amen.

~Your Mother Memories~

~Your Prayer of Praise~

~A Scripture of Encouragement~

TWENTY-TWO: Sorrow Brings Back a Kind Friend

Make me to hear joy and gladness; that the bones which thou hast broken may rejoice.

—Psalm 51:8 KJV

I called my longtime friend, Susie, whom I had exchanged letters with but hadn't spoken to in many years. After telling her about Joshua, she consoled me and encouraged me to cling in the Lord.

In another phone conversation, Susie offered to make us some memorabilia's. "If you'll pick out a few of Joshua's clothes and send them, I'll be happy to make two lap quilts."

Tears creased my lashes. "This is so kind of you, Susie."

Within a few days, I chose two pairs of Joshua's jeans, a pair of corduroys, and several shirts. Those were the clothes I could bear to see turned into squares within quilts. I boxed them and sent them to Susie.

Life became busy for Susie, and she asked her mother to help her complete the quilts.

When I thought about the painstaking work she was doing, my eyes misted. I could hardly wait to have the lap quilts in my hands.

Truly, her work was a labor of love.

Father, friends like Susie are a blessing. I pray I'm as faithful a friend to her. Through Jesus our Lord, Amen.

A Mother's Memories

The crippling effects of Joshua's arthritis had settled in, and we would celebrate his nineteenth birthday in just four months.

He and his friends were looking forward to their first year of college in the fall, but Joshua's dreams unraveled. A few of his buddies noticed and decided on a surfing trip with Joshua to Santa Barbara, California.

Unable to surf for months, Joshua said "no" to their invitation. This handful of buddies from high school, who were a part of the bigger group known as *The Crew*, wouldn't hear of it.

They insisted they would help Joshua get on his board so he could float and take in some sun. Because Joshua had been depressed, I was grateful for these young men.

When Joshua was packed and ready to go, a car pulled into our driveway. I hugged my son good-bye. He left the house, using a cane to ease the pain where ankylosing had fused one side of his pelvis.

One young man jumped from the front passenger seat and strapped Joshua's surfboard onto the car with the other boards.

A tall, wiry boy hauled Joshua's duffle bag from the porch and stuffed it in the trunk. The kid who got out of the front seat hollered, "You take shotgun, Josh."

No one helped Joshua as he eased into the seat, propping his cane next to his leg.

A man wouldn't care for this kind of attention, and they understood.

Their display of love toward Joshua, who was one of the first of *The Crew* who'd become wounded in the battle of life, touched this mother's heart.

Lord God, thank you for having kept my son safe on the ocean waters. I'm glad Joshua had The Crew as his group of friends in his short life. In the dear name of Jesus, Amen.

~Your Mother Memories~

~Your Prayer of Praise~

~A Scripture of Encouragement~

TWENTY-THREE: An Image

It is a good thing to give thanks unto the LORD, and to sing praises unto thy name, O most High.

—Psalm 92:1 KJV

Because of Joshua's Brazilian and Native American heritage, he had thick, black hair. In our community of Hispanics, I often saw the same hair style in other young men.

Several months after Joshua's death, I called for a repairman to come to my house and fix my leaking dishwasher.

Nothing prepared me for when I opened the door to the repairman's knock. I gasped, unable to hide my shock.

How could Joshua be standing on my front porch, smiling and wearing an appliance repair shirt?

I blurted out, "You look so much like my son. He passed away a few months ago." Still on my porch, the young man lowered his eyes for one brief moment.

Unwelcomed tears stung and trickled along my cheeks. *Oh, my word!* I'm crying in front of a stranger.

Now, the young man's expression locked with mine. His eyes stared hard, and his smile came with a respectful amount of sorrow.

"Then this must be hard for you, Mrs. Williams."

No apology from his lips, and he didn't cower from this mama's emotions.

What a warm human being.

Nodding, I spoke a few words about what my son had been like.

Reining in my feelings, I cleared my throat and invited him inside.

Clasping my hands to steady them, I discussed the dishwasher with the patient young gentleman.

After he fixed my dishwasher and left, I gulped air as though I had been holding my breath.

"Thank You, God, for bringing me a silhouette of Joshua. Only You could send such a gift."

Trembling, I slid my back down the door to a squatting position.

Breathe, just breathe.

Later in the darkness of my bedroom, I replayed the moment when I opened the door to the young appliance man.

With fresh tears, I praised my Father again for a glimpse of my son in another's face.

Thank You, Father, for sending a soothing balm for this mother's eyes and heart. I'm resting in You through Jesus, Amen.

A Mother's Memory

My twenty-year-old cousin, Brian, came to live with us a few months after thirteen-year-old Joshua started weight training.

Brian, Jason, and Joshua became inseparable, with Brian being the senior in age. Joshua admired him and wanted to spend his free time learning more about pumping iron with his cousin.

The three boys became more like brothers within those months Brain lived with us, always hanging out in the garage in their spare time using the weightlifting equipment.

The very essence of kindness, Brian was always well-mannered. By example, he helped to mold Joshua into a more respectful teen.

Since Joshua's memorial, Brian has been an important support. He's been wounded, also, and Joshua would be glad for Brian's continued contact with me.

Brian: another blessing from many whom God saw fit to bring into my life.

Father, thank You, for giving me another friend in Brian. I've seen the anguish in his eyes over the loss of his buddy and cousin, Joshua. Please, help Brian to remember the good memories the boys shared. In Christ's holy name, I ask, Amen.

~Your Mother Memories~

~Your Prayer of Praise~

~A Scripture of Encouragement~

TWENTY-FOUR: "LOVE TRUTH"

Beware lest anyone cheat you through philosophy and empty deceit, according to the tradition of men, according to the basic principles of the world, and not according to Christ. For in Him dwells all the fullness of the Godhead bodily.

—Colossians 2:8, 9 NKJV

Going through Joshua's personal things, I found his cigar box.

Memories flooded to the day Joshua and I went to town so Joshua could shop at a cigar store. He bought one cigar, and the clerk gave him an empty, although fancy, cigar box.

Now, my hand trembled as I lifted the lid.

Fingers brushed the top layer of objects, all of them significant to my son. Touching through the treasures, a wadded paper sat buried on the bottom.

My heart quickened. Did I find more words to us from him? In bold print Joshua had written "LOVE TRUTH."

"LOVE TRUTH?"

My frenzied questions battered my mind. Where did he get the idea of "LOVE TRUTH?" Why crumple the note with a clenched fist? Was it for me, his mother, to find?

Later, in Joshua's Bible, the one he handed me before he shot himself, I found a sticky note where he marked Colossians 2:8 and 9

I believe Joshua meant for me to read this passage marked in his Bible.

Oh, my Lord, I'm on a quest to live out "LOVE TRUTH." Teach me Your Word. Help me to grow spiritually to please and honor You. In the holiness of Jesus, I ask, Amen.

A Mother's Memories

Joshua loved high-school debate class.

He had always enjoyed a good argument, searching out other people's ideas and disregarded or included them as his own. Debates lit a flame of excitement under Joshua and pushed him to search for truth.

Since finding Joshua's "LOVE TRUTH" note, I've determined to love truth and embrace it, seeking God's Scriptures daily. I will keep watch and ask God's forgiveness for when my soul believes a falsehood.

Lies and truth cannot reside in the same heart.

This is what I believe about the "LOVE TRUTH" note: Joshua jotted down the words after reading Colossians 2:8 and 9. Later, he crumbled it in self-disgust.

As Joshua wrote in the good-bye letter to me, he regretted choices he made in reckless moments of his youth. He saw himself as a failure, with no hope left and blamed himself to the point of being unforgivable.

He believed Satan's fib.

On Joshua's gravestone, we instructed the carver to inscribe "LOVE TRUTH."

Father, I'm sad for how my son suffered. I'm grateful for the "LOVE TRUTH" note, evidence of his thoughts. I'll cherish his block letters. In the blessed name of Jesus, Amen.

~Your Mother Memories~

~Your Prayer of Praise~

~A Scripture of Encouragement~

TWENTY-FIVE: A Mother's Day Tea

But his mother kept all these sayings in her heart.
—Luke 2:51 KJV

My dear friend, Becky, called me on the phone. "I'm having a Mother's Day tea, and I'm inviting some of our writer friends."

My heart sank. Less than two months into my grief, how could I possibly get through an afternoon without sobbing?

Oh. My. "This would be nice, Becky, but I'll cry, and it will bother people."

"It's in your honor." Her voice rose with a lilt.

Tears stung, and a knot formed in my throat.

"It's hard right now, Jean, but you're a mother, and you need to celebrate your motherhood."

Unknown to Becky, as she talked, droplets of tears coursed onto my lap.

"It'll be fun," she continued, "and everybody will wear their favorite spring hat. I'll make lots of goodies," her voice urged. "And some fabulous peach tea."

My voice quivered. "I do like peaches."

"This will be so good, Jean." Now her voice was happy again. "You'll see."

"This is sweet of you, Becky, but I'm still afraid I'll cry and make everyone uncomfortable."

"Invite Jami and her daughters. We can't leave them out."

Perhaps I could do this with Jami at my side.

When my girls and I arrived at the tea, Becky kept her word. She prepared a long table with a spread of delicious finger foods and sweet treats.

I drank cups of peach tea and made small talk with friends and Jami, and life felt more normal.

All the while, Becky served us, took pictures, and her eager smile melted the rest of my apprehensions.

Weeks later, she surprised me with a photo album of my Mother's Day tea. This truly was another joyful gift for a broken heart.

Thank You, Father God, for the blessings of godly friendships. In Jesus's holiness, I'm grateful, Amen.

A Mother's Memories

A freshman in high school, Joshua placed an oblong gift-wrapped present on the table in front of me.

He bowed his head, showing he worried I might not like it.

"Happy Mother's Day," he said, without even a hint of a smile.

I grinned. "Oh, thank you, Son."

As I tore at the paper on top, Joshua rubbed his finger and thumb together in anticipation.

"I made it in woodshop."

My own fingers worked faster in my accelerated excitement. "I love crafted gifts."

I gasped. "Oh, Joshua." In blue paint, he had printed "MOM'S BOX" on the front below the hinged lid. "You made me a box to store things."

"Actually, Mom, it's for your recipes." He pointed. "I measured with a 5" X 7" recipe card and made the box a bit wider."

"What a great job, honey."

I reached over and gave Joshua a hug and pats on his back.

"You're a fine woodworker, and I'll always cherish this. Thank you."

A soft smile creased his lips. "You're welcome."

I love my shellacked recipe holder for many reasons—one being it has a flaw.

Below the lid, the front has a crack about one-third over. To compensate, when Joshua wrote "MOM'S BOX," he painted his letters to the right of the split in the wood.

He wrote "MOM'S" and below this, "BOX," so the letters are neatly to one side.

Flawed. Like Joshua.

As I was, being his mother.

Dear Father, after twenty-two years, "MOM'S BOX" still sits on a counter in the kitchen. The bright-blue letters, and the ease with which the lid opens, is a reminder of Joshua's handiwork. How blessed to have been loved by him. I'm honored You chose me for his mom. Through Jesus's steadfast love, Amen.

~Your Mother Memories~

~Your Prayer of Praise~

~A Scripture of Encouragement~

TWENTY-SIX: First Overnight with a Granddaughter

For you, O Lord, are my hope, my trust, O Lord, from my youth.
—Psalm 71:5

In the rotation of Jami's three daughters to spend the night at our house, it was Lynsey's turn.

Holding off Lynsey's visit because of my ever-continuing tears, I told Jami at one point, "Honey, I don't want to expose Lynsey to my crying spells. It will upset her. She's already sad over Joshua's death."

Later, Jami called after giving Lynsey my message. "Mom, Lynsey told me this: 'It's okay if Nana cries. It won't bother me.'"

I agreed to have her for a sleep over but was still concerned.

Lynsey settled into our home for her overnight with Nana and Papa.

When I prayed with her at bedtime, tears ran along my cheeks. Ignoring the innocent response she had given to her mom, I shook my head.

"I'm sorry, Lynsey, for being a crybaby. Please don't worry because I'm sad."

Pursing her lips, Lynsey's eyes bore into mine. "Nana, it's okay." She cupped my hands with her own. "I always feel better after I've cried."

From the mouth of an eight-year-old.

Not understanding why, Lynsey's grown-up-like speech made me even more determined to shield her from my sorrow.

For the rest of her visit, I prayed for the Lord God to fill me with His strength so my tears would not fall. He honored my request.

After a few false starts, I learned to stay in the present when the three granddaughters took turns for overnights at Nana and Papa's. We played board games, laughed, and made their favorite foods.

In the process of all this, we discovered the grandchildren needed our company as much as we needed theirs.

They, also, mourned for their beloved uncle Joshy. I believe the girls noticed the sadness in our eyes and understood it was okay for them to feel this raw sorrow of loss.

There was a balance for all of us when we were together: tears, joy, and laughter.

Those times with them blessed my husband and me. The children gave us hope for a future—their future.

Father, thank You for giving me a wise granddaughter. She understands tears cleanse and heal the heart. In the name of Jesus, Amen.

A Mother's Memories

Twenty-five year-old Joshua wrote in his journal:

I tried to be independent. I wanted independence, but I failed, for I felt so alone.

Eight and a half months before his death, Joshua rented a studio apartment. We didn't see much of him at first.

Later, he began eating at our house and sometimes slept on the sofa.

Always happy to see him, I did become alarmed, however, when Joshua stayed almost full-time at our house.

It was obvious he was not adjusting to living on his own.

I never berated Joshua for his long visits at home. He had no social life or job because of his arthritic disability.

As a family, we dined out frequently with Joshua, and afterward, we rented a movie everyone wanted to watch.

My most treasured memories, though, were of the last year with Joshua when we ate lunches together.

We'd eat at our favorite restaurant, and he always relaxed and talked.

Our discussions included politics, his nieces and nephews, and even about the next fix-it project I had planned for the house so we could sell it and retire in Oregon.

My youngest child attempted to live somewhat in normalcy, but his life slid sideways.

Oh, Lord God, I miss my son. I'm sorry Joshua could not live independently. But, I'm glad he knew he could come back home. The empty nest we now experience daily feels extra empty, because of the way Joshua left us. In Jesus's glorious name, please continue to comfort us, Amen.

~Your Mother Memories~

~Your Prayer of Praise~

~A Scripture of Encouragement~

TWENTY-SEVEN: June

Restore to me the joy of your salvation, and uphold me with a willing spirit.

—Psalm 51:12

Pushing away the full plate the waitress set before me, I scowled. "Who in the world wants processed cheese on their nachos?"

"I'm sorry." The new young waitress's smile faded. "But this is the only kind of cheese we have."

"You're telling me you don't have cheddar cheese in this restaurant?"

Cocking one brow, I glared at her in disbelief. "Because I know you do."

I pounded my index finger near my placemat. "I've eaten it right here at this table dozens of times."

The waitress's lips trembled. "Well, yes, ma'am, but I mean, uh, this is the kind of cheese we use for nachos." She nodded yes.

"This is junk-food cheese." I pushed the meal toward her. "Please take this back and make my nachos with cheddar cheese."

Pursing her lips, she left with my plate.

The anger stage clawed its way into my ugly heart, making itself at home in my soul.

A growly, grief-stricken mama.

Questions strangled me. Why did Joshua do this to us? Did he not know this would ruin our lives?

How could he be so selfish?

104

After the nacho meal, my bout of anger exploded with a solid kick to our entry-way closet door.

Yelling in the living room, I hurled my fists at the ceiling.

"I've been convicted and sent to prison for a crime I did not commit."

I glared at the door I dented. "I hate this—my life."

I was angry at Joshua and felt guilty for this, all in one volatile emotion.

"I miss Joshua. I'm sick of crying and tired from not sleeping."

Hugging my chest, the ache beneath my rib pounded.

Father, I cannot stand myself. Please, help! I need Jesus's blessed peace, Amen.

A Mother's Memories

The rake handle struck my nose, and Joshua roared in laughter.

I frowned, covering my face with a hand, while Joshua held his stomach and pointed.

"It's not funny," I said with a pout, and my nose was hot to the touch. With Joshua still doubled over giggling, I snapped at him. "My nose hurts, Josh."

He calmed his laughter long enough to say, "This is the funniest thing I've ever seen, Mom. A real comedy skit."

He pantomimed what happened. "She steps on the rake tines and 'bop,' the handle hits her on the nose." He reared backward and covered his face and guffawed.

I stomped past him and into the house. Tears stung my eyes as I peered into the mirror. A Rudolf nose reflected back at me.

When was the last time Joshua laughed?

Within the mirror's image, the crease between my brows softened. "It was worth it," I whispered.

On the way from the hall bathroom, we met and I touched Joshua's arm. "I must have looked funny, huh?"

Joshua beamed, like he used to before pain overruled his life. "It was classic, Mom, just classic."

Later as I lay in bed, I thanked God my accident gave my son a reason to feel joy.

Little did I know Joshua would laugh only once more.

In a few short months, Joshua took his own life.

Father, I'm glad my son had laughter in his day, but I miss him. In Jesus, Amen.

~Your Mother Memories~

~Your Prayer of Praise~

~A Scripture of Encouragement~

TWENTY-EIGHT: The Urge to Cut Myself

Attend to me, and answer me; I am restless in my complaint and I moan.

—Psalm 55:2

Within months after Joshua's suicide, I experienced a morbid fascination with the kitchen knife blade.

Too often, when I used a sharp knife, I had an urge to slice my forearm. "Lord, these horrid urges have to stop."

Shuddering, my hand forced the knife on to its proper job: to dice the carrots for a stew.

Cutting was not the answer to relieve one's grief.

"Father, please help me. You can take away these thoughts, for they are not mine and they are not wanted. Through the name of Jesus, I ask, Amen."

During this difficult time, I prayed this prayer daily.

Several days later, I withdrew a knife from its sheath to prepare a meal.

And the compulsion to cut myself? Gone.

Father, my emotional sorrow was so unbearable at times. Thank You for saving me from myself. Through Christ's holiness, I'm relieved, Amen.

A Mother's Memories

Joshua came into the house after checking on his ten-year-old Rottweiler, Harloe. "I've got to put him down."

Right then, I sighed, relieved the old guy would no longer suffer. At least Joshua still had another dog to love and care for, Harloe's son, Heinrich.

"I'm sorry, Son." I touched Joshua's arm. "Do you want me to call our vet?"

Joshua shook his head. "No."

Turning off the kitchen sink water, I stared at him.

"What do you mean?"

He kept his eyes averted. "I'm doing this myself."

I gripped his shoulder, but he moved away. "Son, you can't."

He jerked his head and glared. "He's my dog, Mom." As he walked toward the front door, his anger followed like a dark haze.

"Son, stop." I raised my hands. "Where? How?"

He waved me off and slammed the door behind him.

Sometimes, Joshua stomped on my last nerve.

An hour later, Jami called. "Mom, did you know right now Joshua's digging a hole on my property to bury Harloe?"

"Is this what he's doing? Oh, Jami, this will be too much. He'll have another nervous breakdown if he does this himself."

"I agree, Mom." She sighed, her frustration evident.

My daughter Jami and her husband had five acres in the country. It was the only place Joshua could bury his dog.

I hung up the phone and cried for my son.

A year later, Joshua died by suicide.

Oh, Father, only You knew Joshua's mind-set. This was the saddest day for my son, and he never recovered. In Jesus, I ask, is it possible to recover from the loss of Joshua? Amen.

~Your Mother Memories~

~Your Prayer of Praise~

~A Scripture of Encouragement~

TWENTY-NINE: Father's Day

God is not man, that he should lie, or a son of man, that he should change his mind.

—Numbers 23:19

Anticipating the day of fathers, I grew sick of heart.

My Mother's Day was difficult. No doubt. It was made easier, though, because of Becky's Mother's Day tea. Tears—too many to count.

This feels cruel. I wanted to blame someone.

Other than Lord God. I knew He allowed it, but He didn't do this.

Yes, we still have two children. But the third one's ashes lay inside a gray speckled urn, and sat on our fireplace mantle.

We had no idea Joshua would go to such extremes to rid himself of physical and emotional pain.

Just as Jesus said in John10:11— *The good shepherd lays down his life for the sheep* —a parent who loves his child lays down his life for a daughter or son.

But it was too late.

Lord, I pray You will cover us with Your feathers. Carry us as always. With Jesus's name upon my lips I plead, Amen.

A Mother's Memories

Joshua enjoyed an occasional ride on the passenger's seat of our Harley Davidson motorcycle.

I would ride behind on Jason's Harley, and the four of us took off on road trips.

One excursion turned into an overnight to Monterey Bay. We walked on the wharf and ate clam chowder and fresh fish.

We have photos of this trip, and they mean more to me now than before.

I loved being with my three guys, although, I received plenty of being-the-only-female teasing.

I miss this attention.

The first ride Joshua took he was fifteen and it didn't go well. My three guys rode away for the weekend and met with too much hot sun.

I imagine Joshua's arthritis flared in pain for him to blow the fit he had by the morning of the second day.

"Turn these bikes around, or I'm taking a bus back home."

When I got the call about Joshua's misery, I had news for them.

"You guys do need to get home, anyway. Jami just gave birth to her baby."

This trip wasn't the greatest for my three guys, but it is a fond memory for the two men left in our family.

Father, you knew the sorrow of Your Son's suffering. You felt the pain in Your Father's heart for Your Son. Please bless my two guys, for they are minus one. Move them along on their paths of grief, please. In Christ's holiness, I ask, Amen.

~Your Mother Memories~

~Your Prayer of Praise~

~A Scripture of Encouragement~

THIRTY: My Lord Watches Over Me

Cast thy burden upon the LORD, and he shall sustain thee: he shall never suffer the righteous to be moved.
—Psalms 55:22 KJV

For weeks now, classical music played in my mind every waking moment.

Was I going insane from the loss of Joshua?

I needed to talk to a compassionate listener and called someone who didn't know about Joshua's death: my old high school friend, Mary.

After a bit of chitchat, I said, "Mary, my youngest son Joshua died by suicide."

"Oh, Jean, I'm so sorry. Why do you think he did it?"

It was just like Mary to get to the heart of the question.

After giving Mary the reasons we thought, she said in her soothing voice, "Jean, about three months ago, the Holy Spirit pressed upon my heart to pray for you. And what's odd is I hadn't thought of you in a few years."

"Mary, this is about the time Joshua died."

We talked a while longer, and agreed to stay in touch. Bewildered over God's care for me, I leaned against the counter and wept.

Once again, the Lord showed He stood watch. Even though I had not *felt* His presence since the day Joshua died, blessings proved He would not forget me.

God loves me, His damaged, miserable child.

Father, oh, Father. You are good. You are holy. Please continue to show me Your love. Through Jesus's blessed name, Amen.

A Mother's Memories

My knuckles rapped on Joshua's apartment door. His muffled voice came from within. "Who is it?"

"It's me, Son."

Without opening the door, he said, "What are you doing here? You should have called first."

"I became worried when you wouldn't answer your phone."

I paused, wondering what could be so wrong for Joshua to not let me in. "I've been calling you all week."

Joshua opened his studio door a crack. "Mom, can't you come back?" His face was as pale as a mourning dove's breast.

"Are you okay?" In answer to my question, Joshua threw open the door, and my stomach clenched. Blankets twisted on his bed, and hung over the side.

Clothes were strung everywhere. The bathroom was filthy. Piled dishes hid the kitchen counter.

Shocked at my son's normally tidy place, I couldn't speak. Instead, I tackled the dishes in the sink and cleaned the kitchen, praying for the Lord to show me what was wrong and what to say to comfort my son.

Once my nerves calmed, I was able to talk to Joshua but he would not tell me his problem.

Joshua moved back home within the month, on January 1, 2004. Without any warning, he started bringing home his personal items. He grew more solemn and sad as though resigned to an unspoken decision.

Father, only You could have given my son hope. The day he moved back home, I knew his six months of independence failed. He was shutting out his family, and we could not get through to him. Please help us, for we're devastated. Jesus's name, I beg, Amen.

~Your Mother Memories~

~Your Prayer of Praise~

~A Scripture of Encouragement~

THIRTY-ONE: Fourth of July

Surely I have behaved and quieted myself, as a child that is weaned of his mother: my soul is even as a weaned child.

—Psalm 131:2 KJV

Way ahead of the Fourth of July, I became agitated.

How could I possibly endure several hours of loud bangs, pops, and blasts? My nerves crackling, I still replayed in my mind the shot which ended our son's life.

I searched the internet, found a quiet getaway in Santa Barbara, and reserved a room for one night. The place boasted of no TV or radio, and complete quiet from residents was required.

Relieved, I now longed for the Fourth.

We rode our motorcycle, the first overnight trip since Joshua's death. Burdens eased as the Harley Davidson sped further from the empty space where our son lost his battle.

Arriving at the retreat, I was struck with awe. The building sat tucked behind a knoll, surrounded and intertwined with majestic oaks, whose branches reached and curled. Nature's art.

After checking in, I went to the room. Near the door, a canopy of oaks covered the area and down the hill. A soft breeze waved over the place.

With benches situated every few yards on the compound, they became my seats of reflection. Crying once, I sighed a lot, and my heart and my soul rested.

Later in the evening, one muffled firework popped a long ways in the distance.

Lord, You gave me this blessed time on a hillside retreat. You knew how much I could withstand and, at this moment, You allowed a respite from my continual weeping. Thank you. In the name of Jesus, Amen.

A Mother's Memories

Right after Joshua neared the end of his first semester of college, we sat together one evening watching a funny movie.

His shoulders shook in what I supposed was laughter.

Glancing his way, I gasped. "Son, what is it?" My nineteen-year-old's expression distorted with his sobs. I touched his arm. "Please, tell me."

Catching his breath, he said, "Something's wrong with me, Mom."

I grabbed his hand, clammy in my own. "Are you sick?"

"Last week, driving from the school, the last thing I remember was stopping for a red light. Then, after miles down the road, it was like I woke up."

His weeping became a wail.

I wrapped my arm around his shoulders. "Shh, shh," I whispered and my insides trembled.

He slid his arm across the dampness of his face. "That's not all." He cried, again, and then gained his composure.

"I'm blanking out in class, too. After sitting down, before I know it, kids are getting up from their desks because it's time to leave. I don't remember anything the teacher said."

A knot of fear clenched at me like fists. *Joshua's in trouble.* Didn't this happen to people who were under extreme stress?

We talked for a long while, neither one of us willing to leave the other.

Then I said, "Son, we'll tell your dad tomorrow. Maybe he can help. Okay?"

Joshua heaved a sigh. Having turned off the TV long ago, I asked, "Why don't you get some sleep."

The next morning a decision was made.

Jami, Joshua, and I went to a cabin in the mountains for a few days. And, the fresh air and calm of the woods helped Joshua to rest, but he was also too quiet.

Within a few weeks after our return home, Joshua quit college. This began for him the long road of uncertainty of where his life would go from there.

Dear Lord, our family was concerned for this son and brother. We couldn't imagine how he must have suffered, but we walked the path with him as much as he would allow. Through Jesus's holy name, Amen.

~Your Mother Memories~

~Your Prayer of Praise~

~A Scripture of Encouragement~

THIRTY-TWO: A Compassionate Friend

And your ears shall hear a word behind you, saying, "This is the way, walk in it," when you turn to the right or when you turn to the left.

—Isaiah 30:21

After Margaret gave me the phone number to call our local chapter of *The Compassionate Friends*, it took several months before I gathered enough courage.

Beforehand, I began taking their newsletter. Later I called the chapter leader, Eva.

In our conversation, she told me her son died by suicide, also, and we made plans to meet at a park.

On the appointed day, we greeted each other with a common-bond hug and sat on the deep green lawn.

Half an hour into our visit, I trusted her to share my greatest fear.

I leaned forward within a whisper's space. "Eva, I'm going insane." I waited for her shocked expression or a gasp.

Instead, she gave me a knowing look.

"My husband and I felt the same way at first, and it will pass."

But she doesn't know me. How can she be sure? "Why does this happen?"

"It's the struggle to comprehend you will never see your child again. And, from lack of sleep and all the sorrow we feel every waking moment. Our brains become muddled and confused."

She explained we now must live with our new normal—life without our children.

Eva's honesty about how she felt when her son died validated what I dealt with on a daily basis.

I left the park, embracing this idea called a New Normal.

Father, another blessing in the midst of tragedy. Thank You for allowing Eva to come into my life at this perfect and most needed moment. In Christ, I'm grateful, Amen.

A Mother's Memories

"Nosh's mom, Nosh's mom, it's me, Sean."

Five weeks after Joshua's suicide, I was at a restaurant with my daughter Jami to celebrate her birthday. My gaze lifted from the lunch menu and toward the voice.

The disabled young man waved his arms at me from two booths over and hurried to meet us. I stood. "Hi, Sean, how are you?"

Sean's teeth flashed in a childlike grin. "I'm doin' good, Nosh's mom," he said, not once taking his bright expression off of my face. Then he asked, "How's Nosh doin'?"

My chest constricted, and my breath hiccupped. "He's doing better than ever, Sean." What else could be said to protect the innocent boy?

Sean's mouth opened wider, and his voice raised an octave, "Oh, this is good. You tell Nosh ol' Sean says hi." He waved and left.

At the table, I bowed my head. Jami leaned closer to me. "Mom, who is he?"

I whispered, "I can't believe it. This boy, Sean—he's the one who nicknamed Joshua *Nosh*."

Jami gasped. "Really?" I nodded. "But, Mom, how does he know Josh?"

I rubbed my temple with a finger. "Remember when Joshua's arthritis became so painful he couldn't take PE for one semester in his sophomore year?"

"Yes."

I spread my hands before me on the table.

"To get credit for PE, Josh assisted in the special-education class. I'll never forget the day he started talking about a boy named Sean. They became friends, but Sean couldn't say Joshua's name. It always came out Nosh."

Dabbing my eyes with a cloth napkin, I was not one to believe in chance meetings.

"Pretty soon the nickname got around within Joshua's circle of friends in *The Crew*, and they started calling him Nosh."

Now, God gave us the gift of a glimpse into Joshua's past.

Lord, oh, Lord. On the difficult day of celebrating Jami's birthday without Joshua, You gave Jami and me a present. You allowed us to see the disabled boy who loved Nosh. So grateful in Jesus, Amen.

~Your Mother Memories~

~Your Prayer of Praise~

~A Scripture of Encouragement~

THIRTY-THREE: Joshua's Apple Land

My flesh and my heart faileth: but God is the strength of my heart, and my portion forever.

—Psalm 73:26 KJV

I needed to march forward in my grieving, but at the same time, I grew fearful of the idea.

To move on meant to forget Joshua, but this sounded like betrayal.

I stood next to the apple tree on the patio as this war struggled within my heart.

I hated my existence: misery and needing my son.

This mama could no longer see, touch, or be in communication with her child.

I longed to kiss the shiny place on his forehead.

A breeze drifted through the yard, stirring a hint of fall.

"God, help me," I begged.

Not prone to idle hands, I grabbed the garden hose and watered the apple tree. Standing under the tree, I scowled.

It never gave us but a few underdeveloped apples in a season.

My heart drove me back to the dilemma and I whispered, "Lord, You haven't forsaken me, but it feels as though You have."

My convoluted feelings. *I'm so messed up.*

Right then, my shoulder thumped against a smooth object. I bent my neck underneath the tree.

Dozens and dozens of Red Delicious apples dangled, filling in the branches.

I gasped. "How did I miss all these?"

Then I remembered Joshua watered the tree the year before until it almost drowned.

Joshua knew what he was doing with this barren tree, and now we had an abundance of baseball-sized apples.

Father, thank You for giving us this bounty of fruit. In Jesus's name, I'm glad to see Joshua's efforts have lived on, Amen.

A Mother's Memories

Less than a year before he died, Joshua watered our apple tree often.

I doubted the watering he did would help, because the tree had never given us much fruit.

One morning, Joshua watered for a full hour. I shook my head and came outside to discuss the cost of his efforts. I ended my speech with, "Son, I think you're over watering."

He kept his eyes on the spray. "What makes you think this?"

I pointed at the ground. "You're flooding the tree, and the water bill is too high."

"Mom," Joshua said in his patient voice, "this tree needs to drink, or it won't give fruit."

Beneath its branches a huge mud puddle grew. "All right, Son, but I don't agree." I walked back into the house mumbling.

Sometimes there's no changing his mind.

Joshua ignored my not agreeing comment. Of course, he kept flooding the silly tree.

Lord, I grew more impatient with Joshua. Now You are teaching me patience of a different kind: living without my son. I need mercy. In Christ's holy name, Amen.

~Your Mother Memories~

~Your Prayer of Praise~

~A Scripture of Encouragement~

THIRTY-FOUR: A Respite in the Mountains

To shew forth thy lovingkindness in the morning, and thy faithfulness every night.

—Psalm 92:2 KJV

"Yes, I'll help after the baby's birth."

It was mid-July, and I reserved train tickets online. In a few days I would sway on the tracks toward my home state of Oregon.

Was I truly leaving this house—the place where my son died four months ago—if only for a few weeks?

Arriving in the wilderness setting Jason and his family called home, he offered for me to sleep in a small one-room cabin with no electricity or plumbing.

"The trail is not too awful long, Mom," Jason said, "if you want to stay out there."

I hugged him. "I'll take it."

The first night was a bit scary, but I always loved a challenge with nature. I had never been alone in the dark in the middle of the forest.

A flashlight as my beacon, I climbed into the comfy bed. Once settled, I switched off the light and slept.

A wild, high-pitched bark-scream woke me from a deep and vivid dream. My neck tingled.

What could it be?

When I mentioned it the next morning, Jason told me it was a fox.

Knowing this didn't frighten me when the creature sang his call the following night.

Contented, I sighed and listened to the wild song from inside the safety of the cabin.

I slept in the cabin a few more times until the baby came, and then I stayed closer to help the family.

This new grandbaby was colicky, and I walked a path outside to give her family a much needed break.

Father, thank You for the three weeks spent in the wild with my grandchildren. In awe, I witnessed the birth of my granddaughter. I'm grateful for the time of rest, also. In Jesus's comfort, Amen.

A Mother's Memories

"Mrs. Williams, if the baby doesn't come in the next push, we'll have to prep you for a cesarean section."

My heart skipped. "No, Doctor, I can do this." I craned my neck to speak to my birth coach. "Are you ready?"

Instinctively, my coach grabbed two pillows and placed them low behind my back to elevate me.

The doctor's voice broke the anticipation among us. "Here comes another contraction. *Push!*"

Go, go, go.

I bore down with the last of my strength. Propelled from behind to an upright position, I pushed with my feet.

My little one slid into the physician's hands. "It's a boy." I collapsed onto the bed and stretched my arms for my baby. "Let me have him."

The doctor laid him next to my heart. I crooned soft words to my long-awaited child with coal-black hair like his sister Jami's.

Dear Lord, this son was a perfect gift. Thank You for the strength and determination to birth this child naturally and without pain medication. Through Your Son's holy name, I praise You, Amen.

~Your Mother Memories~

~Your Prayer of Praise~

~A Scripture of Encouragement~

THIRTY-FIVE: Becky and the Writing Project

I am weary with my groaning; all the night make I my bed to swim; I water my couch with my tears.

—Psalm 6:6 KJV

"What you need is a book writing project, Jean."

My friend, Becky, sounded determined.

First she held the Mother's Day tea in my honor, and now this.

My lips curved upward, and I pressed my ear closer to the phone.

She inhaled on the other end of the phone line.

"I've decided we're doing a children's book of Bible stories. You create the in-your-own-words stories from Scripture verses. I'll tie in with how the readers can apply each story to their lives."

I straightened the slump of my shoulders.

"Really, Becky? We can work together?"

She published hundreds of books in her career, and I would learn from her professionalism.

"Sure. Let's start right away."

The project took several months, and I enjoyed every moment of our working relationship. Becky was a patient teacher, and her skills improved my writing as I had hoped.

I'm grateful Becky set aside some of her busy schedule to keep me occupied in an otherwise miserable and confused new way of life.

Lord God, You threw the lifeline of a kind friend, and I grabbed and hung on. Always the healer, You are a help in time of trouble. In Jesus, I thank You, Amen.

A Mother's Memories

As a young toddler, Joshua became interested in Bible stories before bedtime.

Wouldn't you know his favorite was the one about David and Goliath? After I read the story, Joshua would beg, "Tell it, again, Mama."

His siblings and I would settle in for another reading to bring a sought-out smile upon Joshua's face.

In the back of the book, there were questions to ask the children, to see if they grasped the story. I would read one and whoever raised their hand first gave the answer.

We had great fun when Joshua would say, "I know, I know," and gave another toddler's version like "banged the giant on the head."

And, Joshua would smack his own forehead with his palm.

The older children covered their mouths and giggled. I pursed my lips to suppress a grin.

"Yes, Joshua, this happened, but you didn't answer the question I asked."

Now, his sister and brother laughed, and one of them told Joshua the answer. Soon enough, Joshua comprehended the stories and answered my questions correctly.

And we were proud of our little guy.

Father, what an adorable child You gave to us. Even at an early age, Joshua loved to act out with earnest hand and body motions. Bless You, Holy Father, for giving us this son. In Christ's holy name, Amen.

~Your Mother Memories~

~Your Prayer of Praise~

~A Scripture of Encouragement~

THIRTY-SIX: A Panic Attack

Create in me a clean heart, O God; and renew a right spirit within me.

—Psalm 51:10 KJV

At over the six month mark, I swallowed fear as it rose in my throat.

"I can't take in a full breath."

We were sitting at a steakhouse restaurant and my friend nodded.

"You're having a panic attack."

I pressed a palm to my chest. "Oh."

Many panic attacks followed in the months ahead. They left me breathless and out of sorts. And still, most of my thoughts revolved around Joshua.

How could I go on without ever seeing my son again? And, why wasn't anyone talking about Joshua? Jami did. Mona said his name without pause.

I'd think, "Please, people, continue the conversation when I mention my son's name."

Is this so hard?

And when I considered if I were happy? No, I couldn't imagine a joy-filled life in my future.

The person I once was died with Joshua. This was my New, Wretched Normal.

Father Lord, I feel isolated. Folks mean well, but this mama needs to hear her son's name from their mouths. And please help me, Lord, for the panic attacks are suffocating. In the name of Jesus, I beg, Amen.

A Mother's Memories

I waited for the perfect moment to spy in Joshua's bedroom.

He stayed in there all the time—a few months before he died. He kept his door shut, hiding something from us.

Joshua went into the bathroom carrying his backpack.

I seized this opportunity to snoop.

I turned the knob, stepped inside, and jerked backward. Joshua had covered the cracks in the knotty pine which covered the bottom half of the walls with masking tape.

I shut the door to the gloom. A person who was frightened to the extreme would do this.

Joshua's psychiatrist was not helping him. I was certain he needed to see a Christian therapist, one who could possibly help him wean off of or prescribe medications which actually worked.

Wondering how approachable he'd be, I hoped Joshua would listen to reason.

Dear God, I didn't know what was best. I feared Joshua would leave if I brought up the need to change to a therapist. I hesitated and then it was too late. With Jesus as my only comfort, I was so sad for Josh, Amen.

~Your Mother Memories~

~Your Prayer of Praise~

~A Scripture of Encouragement~

THIRTY-SEVEN: Classical Music in my Mind

My soul is also sore vexed: but thou, O LORD, how long?
—Psalm 6:3 KJV

At almost the seventh month after Joshua's death, every morning when I woke, classical music still played in my head.

Even though I enjoyed Beethoven, I hadn't been listening to his symphonies. It was too painful, for this was Joshua's favorite music.

Was the lady from *The Compassionate Friends* correct? Would I be okay? Or could someone go insane from the tears and sorrow?

What was God thinking to allow me to suffer so horrifically? For one of my greatest fears had come true: the loss of one of my children.

One morning, I walked outside and picked a daisy. Plucking its petals, my voice was filled with melancholy.

"God loves me, He loves me not." At the last two petals, I pulled them both. "He loves Jean."

Not long after, my friend Mona and I met at a café. As she had before, she reassured me I was doing well sloshing through the path of grief.

From across the table I said, "But my mind keeps hearing classical music. Something has to be wrong with me."

Gentle Mona set down her fork next to her pie plate. For a moment she stared across the room, no doubt forming the perfect words to comfort me.

She met my gaze and pronounced, "Well, Jean, we have to fill our minds with something, and classical music is soothing."

Lord, You do love me. You gave me Mona, a new friend, a few months before Joshua died. She's been willing to hold my hand through this journey of misery. I'm grateful to You for her. In Christ, I'm still sad, though, Amen.

A Mother's Memories

"Would you like to attend a Beethoven concert with me, Son?"

Seventeen-year-old Joshua's eyes brightened. "Yeah, this would be neat."

As a youngster, Joshua took piano lessons. He caught on with ease and enjoyed the Beethoven music.

At a first recital, though, he fumbled his playing on more than a few notes.

Nervous, Joshua's brows and shoulders rose as he paused. Sighing, he continued where he'd left off.

After the next piano lesson, Joshua entered the house. "I don't want to play anymore."

My dish-toweled hand stilled its drying on a plate. "What? But why?"

"I don't like recitals, and the teacher says I have to do them."

"Then keep practicing at home and learn on your own."

"No." Joshua stuck his head in the refrigerator. "I want to learn a new instrument."

A few years later, and after never touching a piano key again, he chose the guitar.

This didn't keep him from listening to Beethoven, though.

Until he left us.

Father, how I miss listening to music with my son. In Jesus's blessed name, my heart aches, Amen.

~Your Mother Memories~

~Your Prayer of Praise~

~A Scripture of Encouragement~

THIRTY-EIGHT: Help Me to Rest

In peace I will both lie down and sleep; for you alone, O LORD, make me dwell in safety.

—Psalm 4:8

At three in the morning, I sat on our sofa in the darkened living room with my head bowed.

Night after night, I did this.

The next day at the vitamin section of my favorite natural foods store, I waited for someone to help me.

A lady about my height clasped her hands before her. "Can I answer a question?"

I told her I had not slept well for seven months.

She raised her index finger. "I've got the solution."

Relief washed over me, for I wanted to believe.

Later, before bed, I took the magnesium along with my normal calcium supplement and did not wake for hours.

A big change from the mere three hours of broken sleep.

Once again, Lord, you rescued me when I needed it the most. You created the natural mineral which helps with sleep. Through Jesus's name, I praise You, Amen.

144

A Mother's Memories

"Son, I believe if you build up your immune system, your arthritis pain will lessen or disappear."

"This makes sense." Joshua arched his brows. "How do I start?"

After visiting the library to do some research, we implemented an agreed upon health plan. Joshua ate healthy foods, added supplements, and scheduled professional massages, as well as the use of a private spa.

Within two months, Joshua walked without a limp where the arthritis had at one time settled in his foot. The swelling and heat there and on his knuckles disappeared.

Joshua exclaimed one day, "We did it, Mom."

I grinned. "You were a determined patient, Son."

Was it chance a few months before Joshua started his regiment, we moved next door to people who would generously open their private spa to us?

I believe not.

Their spa included a sauna, hot tub, and cold pool with an outside door for our easy access.

A few years later, having not continued the regimen, Joshua's immune system suffered and never recovered.

Thank you, Holy Father, for helping Joshua, as I asked for Your guidance to take away his arthritic pain. The rest was up to him. In Jesus's holy name, I continue to remember, Amen.

~Your Mother Memories~

~Your Prayer of Praise~

~A Scripture of Encouragement~

THIRTY-NINE: Thanksgiving without Joshua

The LORD is good to those who wait for him, to the soul who seeks him.

—Lamentations 3:25

Our extended family sat down to the Thanksgiving meal and held hands around the dining room table.

Everyone waited for the head of our family to pray.

"Why don't we take turns saying what we are grateful for, before I pray."

I gulped. What to say when my time came?

Please, Lord, help me not to cry. Help me to consider others so they will not become upset. This is a hard day for everyone.

Most of the family members said they were grateful for relatives present, and for those who had passed away.

Right before my turn, I shifted in my chair.

Everyone stared at the mother of Joshua. I inhaled. "I'm thankful for the twenty-five years I had with Joshua."

Keeping my head bowed, tears stung the bridge of my nose. Don't cry. Please don't.

After the prayer, everyone said, "Amen."

I sighed softly, so as not to draw attention. Tears fell now as everyone passed the food and filled their plates.

I dabbed at my cheeks with a napkin. *Thank You, Lord.*

Lord, Your strength within me gets me through. For certain, I'm grateful Joshua came to this earth, but not for his death. I'm honored to have had him as my son. In the name of Your Son, Amen.

147

A Mother's Memories

A walloping pain hit my lower back. "Ow!"

From my standing position in the kitchen, I could no longer look down and find my ankles.

Caressing my baby belly, I sighed as the pain eased, and continued to open a can of yams.

What I wanted was to go to bed, for flu-like aches had consumed my body.

My long-awaited child was due any day. Our planned Thanksgiving meal promised simplicity, so much so we would not drive the hour to feast with family.

Our seven-year-old daughter Jami helped me with preparations. She placed the food down as I instructed. With the meal ready we sat at our places to eat.

Being funny, someone said, "Canned ham, canned yams, and canned corn—our Thanksgiving meal from a can."

Right then I winced again, and this time from the baby pressing against my pelvis. It *had* been too much work, but I was the one who wanted a Thanksgiving meal.

I truly was thankful and happy about the baby's upcoming birth.

As we ate, we talked about going for a ride afterward.

With my fork, I moved the food around on my plate. "This would be nice, right guys?" Everyone agreed.

Finished with our dinner, my family cleaned the kitchen while I elevated my puffy feet. Ah, this is my treat.

Four days later before dawn, a powerful bump hit below my stomach. "That smarted."

As the pain calmed, I drifted to sleep. A few hours passed and, at 7:00 a.m., the contractions began and kept me awake. I sucked air through clenched teeth.

By five o'clock the same evening Joshua came into the world.

Our little guy added more love and laughter within our family than I ever could have imagined.

I'm happy I'm the mother of three children, Lord. Thank You. In Jesus's holiness, I'm joyful, Amen.

~Your Mother Memories~

~Your Prayer of Praise~

~A Scripture of Encouragement~

FORTY: Celebrating Joshua's Birthday

The Lord is my portion, says my soul, therefore I will hope in him.
—Lamentations 3:24

Two days after Thanksgiving, Jami and her family arrived early in the evening with a food dish to add to my birthday menu.

She kissed my cheek and wrapped her arms around me, hanging on tight.

"How are you, Mommy?"

My tears welled behind lashes on this special, difficult day. "I'll be okay. Now you're here."

She nodded. "I love you, Mom." And, she went about setting the food out.

After our home-baked meal, we set Joshua's favorite birthday dessert on the table: New Orleans chocolate cake. No candles. No singing.

Quietly, Jami and I sliced and served cake and dished spoonfuls of chocolate ice cream.

One of Jami's girls said, "Uncle Joshy's cake tastes good, Nana." My lips curved upward, tears stinging.

Later, we cleared the leftovers to the breakfast bar, and everyone spread to different locations at two tables.

Piling boxes of puzzles on one table, I spoke to my grandchildren.

"Okay, girls, these are easier puzzles for your age. We adults will help if you want." Most of them chose animal designs and got to work.

At a distance from the table, I crossed my arms. My son-in-law helped two of his children place the puzzle pieces right side up.

Everyone murmured in quiet tones intent on solving puzzles.

It started as an awkward night, celebrating Joshua's birthday without him. It became a relaxed determination to honor him.

Moving to the kitchen, I cleaned dishes, wiped counters, and cried silent tears so as not to disturb my family and their peaceful moment.

Father God, thank You for family willing to gather together even though it's difficult. We miss our Joshua, and nothing we do will return him within our midst. Help us to continue to love one another through these hardest of days. Through Jesus's holy name, I ask, Amen.

A Mother's Memories

Early one morning, months before his death, Joshua stood before me in the kitchen. "Happy Birthday, Mom."

Unsmiling, he pursed his lips and stared at me.

I hugged him. "Thank you, Son, for remembering. Can you believe I'm fifty?"

His eyes darted about. I wondered if mentioning my age worried him.

After a long pause, he finally said, "Yeah, fifty. Dress nice today."

Minutes later, with a duffle bag slung over his shoulder, he opened the front door. "I've got to run an errand."

Okay, something's going on. Changing into a pretty dress, I pondered over Joshua's sad demeanor. I never knew what my son was thinking, and I'd learned from experience not to pry.

Later, our car entered the opened gates of the city park. Picnic areas passed me, and we ended at a dead-end barbecue area with covered seating. A group of people stood around the site.

At first they appeared as strangers, but then faces wore grins. Our cousin and her family walked toward us, with Jami and her family and my closest friend.

People yelled, "Surprise! Happy Birthday."

My hands flew to my cheeks. "Who did this?"

Someone said, "Joshua."

My youngest child stayed at my side throughout the day, except when he discovered he'd left a pot of spaghetti on the counter at the house.

Joshua even stood by while I played volleyball with our cousin's children and our grandchildren.

His face softened and appeared interested as we socked the ball around, so he enjoyed this part.

Other than this, he never smiled, and this niggled at my heart.

In the evening, after I crawled into bed, my mind flashed back to the stern expressions on Joshua's face for most of the day.

He's worried because I'm growing old.

Dear Lord, the day was a mixture of happy and sad. Joshua worked to bring people together for my birthday, and now I understand why. Please, Lord, help me to forgive him, for planning another event which took his life. In Jesus, Amen.

~Your Mother Memories~

~Your Prayer of Praise~

~A Scripture of Encouragement~

FORTY-ONE: Losing a Long-Time Friend

But you, O LORD, are on high forever.

—Psalm 92:8

I punched in my closest friend's phone number and got her answering machine.

Again, after my third attempt to reach her.

Wrinkling my brow, I hung up this time without leaving a message. Why wouldn't she return my calls? Surely, she wasn't avoiding me.

After ten years of heart-to-heart conversations, walks on the sand dunes, and lunches at our favorite restaurant?

I had waited for her to reach out as my birthday came and left.

Now, I waited for her call when her birthday came within a month after mine. Did she forget about our annual birthday lunch celebrated between our birthdates?

Slumping my shoulders and sighing over her silence, I was certain now she no longer wanted my friendship.

When I received her Christmas card in the mail and opened it, I blinked. No "how are you doing?" No glowing words like she used to write.

Is it possible one can be reduced to a Christmas card with only a signature?

I knew her well enough if I had done something wrong, she would have confronted me. A new loss to grieve, I struggled through the stages of sorrow and anger.

How much more could this broken mama withstand?

Much later, I spoke to my hospice therapist about feeling abandoned by someone I thought of as a close friend.

"She was at my fiftieth birthday party, and she came to Joshua's memorial. She was even the last one to leave."

The therapist said, "It's another loss for sure. But some people are uncertain of what to say or do when someone they know suffers a death from suicide."

She shrugged. "Your friend might feel you are better off without her."

Tears trailed along my cheeks. "But I'm not."

The counselor's eyes filled with moisture. "I'm so sorry, Jean."

Father, I'm so sorry also. How could my friend leave our relationship without an explanation? Help me to forgive her, for I'm truly hurt. Through the name of Christ, I ask, Amen.

A Mother's Memories

"Happy birthday, dear Joshua, happy birthday to you. We love you sooo."

Our family clapped and said, "Yea, yea." He smiled and tucked his ear near a shoulder.

Jami said, "Blow out your candle, Joshy." And so he did, with the help of his brother and sister.

It had been a difficult first year for our boy, for he stayed sick with colds and respiratory problems.

He had food sensitivities, and so I settled on making a honey-sweetened banana sheet cake with no frosting. I arranged miniature toys on top for decorations.

Removing the candle, I ruffled his hair. "You're a big one-year-old." I pointed to the toy train. "It's yours, Joshua—take it."

His pudgy hand reached part way and stopped, and then Joshua lifted the train and brought it to his chest. "Mine."

His grin lit our hearts.

Thank You, Father, for enriching our lives with Joshua's presence. In Jesus's holy comfort, Amen.

~Your Mother Memories~

~Your Prayer of Praise~

~A Scripture of Encouragement~

FORTY-TWO: Christmas Baking and Decorating in Joshua's Memory

For he will command his angels concerning you to guard you in all your ways.

—Psalm 91:11

"Nana, please, we have to bake cookies, and you need a Christmas tree to decorate."

Our eldest grandchild, Morgan Ann, would not quit on the topic of Christmas.

I did not want to bake.

The idea of a tree saddened us; Joshua had always been involved with the choosing.

When Morgan pleaded with us more than twice, we relented.

Morgan and her two sisters, Lynsey and Carley, came over on the agreed upon day.

My heart's desire was to hang only handmade ornaments on this year's tree.

Our granddaughters created a mess with glue, glitter, and construction paper.

We decorated cutout egg cartons for bells and strung cranberries and popcorn on strings. The girls hung the ornaments on a three-foot-tall tree.

A welcoming inspiration, Morgan insisted we make Joshua's favorite cookies.

We baked thumbprint cookies, and hand-decorated snowmen, Santa Claus, and angel-figure sugar cookies with pink, red, and green frosting.

My granddaughters howled with laughter over smeared frosting on their faces.

I snapped oodles of pictures which I shall always cherish.

Our granddaughters left in the early evening, and my battered heart beat with a joyful rhythm.

Father, thank You for prompting us to please our granddaughters. We made wonderful memories, and they blessed me. Please bless them as they grow into young women who learn how to follow after You. In the name of Jesus, I ask, Amen.

A Mother's Memories

By age two, Joshua would scoot an extra chair to the table and watch me knead dough for whole grain bread.

He patted and pushed next to my hands. "I wanna help."

First, I washed and dried his hands and stood him in a chair in front of me. I reached around his arms. "Push down like this."

He shoved his palm into the soft dough. "This?"

I dipped my chin. "Yes."

At one point, he said, "It's hard, Mama," and he grunted as his muscles worked. When he lifted his palm, his print left an impression and another on my heart.

Later, as the bread baked, he peered through the oven glass. "Is it ready, Mama?"

"No, not yet."

As the loaves cooled on a rack, Joshua leaned closer and smelled. "Now we can eat?"

Wagging my hand toward his high chair at the table, I said, "Sit down. I'll bring you a piece with butter and jam."

Joshua planted his rump in the seat, and I adjusted the tray over his legs. He folded his hands and waited.

I placed the platter of bread before him. We prayed our "Thank You, God" prayer.

At "amen," my little guy grabbed the bread and chomped into its crunchy warmth. He grinned, crust poking from the corners of his lips.

"Yummy, Mama."

Forward to twenty-one years later.

"Mom," Joshua said, "these buckwheat groats I'm making are turning out good this time."

I peered into the skillet. Sure enough, they were not a gray blob but held their color and even texture.

"Now you'll have to teach me how to make this, Son."

We sat down to a lunch of buckwheat groats and ate the entire batch.

Father, I hold dear the times when my son and I cooked and baked together. In Jesus's glorious name, I'm filled with sorrow and gratitude, Amen.

~Your Mother Memories~

~Your Prayer of Praise~

~A Scripture of Encouragement~

FORTY-THREE: Christmas Day

Let him who walks in darkness and has no light trust in the name of the LORD and rely on his God.

—Isaiah 50:10

Christmas morning I slipped from my bed and planted my feet on the cold, cold floor.

Someone was missing.

My muddled brain ran along the corridors of the all-too familiar emotions.

Sad—why did he go? Did he not love us?

This feeling had taken root and choked me, day after day and throughout the months.

Fearful—the moment the killing shot blasted through Joshua's room. I still can't wrap my mind around life absent of Joshua.

How can there even be this? Without him?

Lonely—I'm wretched. Numerous times, I've prayed for Lord God to stop my heart from beating.

We came through most of the special holidays and events without our son.

And yet, this day—Christmas—was the toughest.

Jami invited us to spend the morning with them and watch the children open their gifts. Much relieved, I accepted.

Normally, Jami and her family had their own family gift-exchange time, and we would meet later in the day at a relatives' home.

At first, we sat on Jami's couch and watched like outsiders.

The children drew us in, though, their Nana and Papa. Their smiles beckoned us as they showed off the gifts they received.

Sorrow filled a pocket of my heart, but—I laughed now at the cute antics of our grandchildren and their goofy grins, bows on heads, and playing with empty boxes as the toys sat untouched on the floor.

We crawled into a hole, Father, not wanting to face this day. We survived, and did not forget You offered up Your Son to save us. Born, died, and resurrected for our sins. In Him, Amen.

A Mother's Memories

"We have one more gift, Joshua, and can you guess who it's for?"

Four-year-old Joshua pointed at his brother. "Jason."

I laid the box at Joshua's feet. "No. It's for you, Son."

Joshua's eyes grew as large as marble shooters.

"Open it, open it," we all sang.

He ripped apart the candy-cane-design paper and looked inside. He sucked in a breath. "Ahhh."

"Sit on the floor and you can hold one." I touched his shoulder.

Joshua smothered his face into the guinea pig fur. "He's so cute, Mom."

"They're both girls." My fingers smoothed down the soft fur.

Weeks later, on a snowy January day, Jami squealed.

"Mom, Mom, come see the guinea pigs."

I ran from my bed-making job and stood over the box. "There are—what?"

I gasped. "Three, four, five?"

Joshua held out his hands. "Can I hold—?"

"Not yet," Jami said, "the babies are too small."

He dropped his arms to his sides. "Okay, Jami."

I nudged Joshua away from what was now a baby nursery box.

"We don't want to upset the mama."

Joshua patted my arm. "Do the babies drink their mama's milk like I used to drink your milk?"

I grinned. "Yes, Son."

He pursed his lips and smiled.

Holy Father, what a wonderful memory. Thank You for all the Christmases we shared as a family. In Jesus's beloved name, Amen.

~Your Mother Memories~

~Your Prayer of Praise~

~A Scripture of Encouragement~

FORTY-FOUR: The Last Firsts of Holidays

If your law had not been my delight, I would have perished in my affliction.

—Psalm 119:92

New Year's Day came with a biting chill, and I cranked up the heat.

My groggy mind. Remembered.

I would still celebrate, keeping with Joshua's and my tradition: hard salami slices and cheese with fancy crackers and olives—his favorite—and sparkling apple cider.

No need to buy two bottles.

One would be enough.

I prayed throughout the day, as was my new habit or rather need. I cried and sang.

Talked in whispers to God, "I'm still missing Joshua, Lord. It feels as though my heart is ripping from my chest. He is my son and my friend."

Around eight o'clock, I made the tray of snacks. Watching a movie, I snuggled next to the fire and worked at forgetting.

Dear God, another celebration behind us. We don't understand why Joshua is gone. Being truthful with You, Lord. Holding on to my Redeemer, Amen.

A Mother's Memories

"Mom." Twenty-one-year-old Joshua called me into his room. "Look what I found."

I entered his bedroom. "What?"

Reaching into his duffle, he grinned. "It's fate." He lifted into the air a gray-and-white cat.

I inhaled a sharp breath.

"You can't bring *that* in here. You know I'm allergic."

The corners of his mouth lifted, and he cradled the young cat to his chest.

"Oh, I know, Mom, she'll live outside. No store bought food for her, because she'll be a mouser."

His brows waggle-danced.

"Don't you want her to kill the mice we've got running all over this place?"

I cocked my head to one side. "She is pretty, but now outside she goes.

A pucker formed between his eyebrows. "She's got to get used to me first or she'll run away."

My back stiffened. "This cat can't stay in the house, Josh."

His hand slid down the cat in a back-and-forth rub. "She'll stay in my room. Just for a few days."

I threw up my hands and left. Over my shoulder I said, "Keep your door shut."

"You won't regret it, Mom. She'll get rid of the mice for you."

Joshua raised his voice as I continued to walk away, "You wait and see."

It took Joshua two years to name our mouser.

Finally he decided on LiahNora. His insistence the cat needed a special name, and the way Joshua spelled it seemed odd.

It still seems so today.

Is there a connection between LiahNora and Joshua's Irish heritage?

I'll never know.

Thank You, Father, for the comfort of LiahNora, who lived eight more years after Joshua died. In our Lord and Savior, Amen.

~Your Mother Memories~

~Your Prayer of Praise~

~A Scripture of Encouragement~

FORTY-FIVE: Valentine's Day

O Lord, open thou my lips; and my mouth shall shew forth thy praise.

—Psalm 51:15 KJV

On Valentine's Day morning, I reminisced last year's Valentine's dinner with Joshua.

We had asked Joshua along and he accepted our invitation. I believe now Joshua knew at the time he would leave us soon. Did he want us to have the memory of the three of us eating at our favorite restaurant?

Or maybe he didn't want left home alone.

Joshua hated the long wait in line, clear outside to the sidewalk. But once we were seated inside, he relaxed and enjoyed the meal.

Of course, Joshua remained quiet, as was his habit in the few years before his death.

Now, I bowed my head and my body quivered with grief.

I vowed to spend the day in prayer, Scripture reading, and thankful praise for the time we had together on Joshua's last Valentine's Day.

Dear Lord, I miss my sweetheart son, our shared meals, and even his quiet demeanor. Most of all, I miss his glorious laughter which grew infrequent until there was nothing left. In my misery, I praise You. Through Jesus's holy name, Amen.

A Mother's Memories

Jami placed the cracker on my bottom lip. "Come on, Mom, you have to eat."

Queasiness gripped me, and I swiped it away. "I'll throw up."

She sighed and walked to where Joshua stood at the end of my bed. "You heard the nurse. Mom can't leave until she eats this."

Joshua held out his fingers. "Let me try." I groaned, closing my eyes.

Standing next to the bed, he said, "Mom, you have to eat this silly cracker or they won't let you out."

Family members in the room chuckled. Joshua's way of putting things almost made me laugh, but I gulped down a wave of nausea.

He held the cracker near my mouth, and his voice rose to a higher note. "Open up."

Joshua deserved credit for his creative efforts, so I nibbled on the tasteless thing. As if this was what they were waiting for, my family decided to leave for lunch.

When Joshua remained at my side, someone asked, "Are you coming, Joshua?"

"I'm staying with Mom." He offered me the second half of the cracker. "Gotta make sure she eats."

Five minutes after they left, the nurse came in and nodded at me while I licked crumbs from my lips.

She said, "Do you have a ride, Mrs. Williams?"

Joshua took a step closer to her. "I'm taking my mom home."

After the forty-five-minute drive, Joshua guided me to our sofa. He placed a glass of water on the coffee table and covered me with a blanket.

Joshua took care of his mom, as I had once nurtured him as a little guy.

Father, I'm grateful for Joshua's presence and his care after my surgery. Thank You for creating my son. In Jesus, Amen

~Your Mother Memories~

~Your Prayer of Praise~

~A Scripture of Encouragement~

FORTY-SIX: Another New Grandbaby

The LORD is good, a stronghold in the day of trouble; he knows those who take refuge in him.

—Nahum 1:7

Eleven days before the first anniversary of Joshua's death, Jami gave birth to her fifth child, Torry John.

Another special event within the first year, our family rejoiced over another baby. And with six granddaughters, we were glad for grandson number three.

Underlined in our minds, we were sad Torry would never know his uncle Joshy. Once again, I was reminded Joshua would miss out on the new babies yet to come into our growing family.

Joshua had enjoyed his Uncle Joshy status. There were nieces and nephews he'd grown closer to because they were older, but he loved each of them.

About a month before Joshua died, he asked Jami if he could babysit her daughters. He hadn't been coming around much, so Jami was surprised but glad for a date night with her husband.

Did Joshua long to spend a few more hours with his nieces before he left them?

Dear Lord, creator of all living beings, thank You for the new baby. Please help us to focus on and be grateful for awesome life and less on death and what we have lost. Through Jesus's holy name I ask, Amen.

A Mother's Memories

"Mom, I want to go see Jason's new baby today."

Jason's baby had been home from the hospital a few days, and Joshua couldn't wait to see his first nephew.

He loved Jami's three daughters, but this was a man thing: Joshua's first nephew, the next generation to carry on the family name.

In Jason's living room, Joshua settled onto the sofa and held baby Jason Jr. He cradled the new child in his arms, as though holding royalty.

Then, he stared at the little guy, so intent it seemed, to memorize each of his features.

After Joshua held baby Jason for half an hour, we left. He didn't say much except he was a cute baby.

We later took a picture of four generations of male Williamses, and Joshua stood next to Jason, who held his son.

Please, Father, guide the remaining males in our family to grow into faithful Christians in Your strength. Through Christ, Amen.

~Your Mother Memories~

~Your Prayer of Praise~

~A Scripture of Encouragement~

FORTY-SEVEN: Gifts from Joshua's Clothes

As in water face reflects face, so the heart of man reflects the man.
—Proverbs 27:19

"Oh, Susie, they are beautiful!"

My dear friend draped across my sofa the lap quilts she made from Joshua's garments.

She created mine from Joshua's jeans and slacks, so it had a pocket with a button.

I chose these clothes because I had cut and sewed the hems of Joshua's new pants before he could wear them.

The quilt made from Joshua's shirts represented the muscle men with broad shoulders in our family.

Also, Susie presented two quilt pillows—one for each sibling, Jami and Jason. Susie spent time with the creations, and the pillows were a surprise for our children.

Susie rose from the living room chair. "I'll see you at the cemetery."

I hugged her and thanked her. "I'm so glad you'll be a part of the first-year anniversary of Joshua's passing. His stone is beautiful."

"You'll bury Joshua's ashes later?"

I nodded. "Tomorrow. A few family members will come. No children, except for the two eldest granddaughters."

After Susie left, I finished the preparations of Joshua's favorite foods to bring for the reception after the graveside services.

A day I didn't want to see come. A day I longed to have over.

Father, please help me get through this second memorial. Thank You for blessing me with several loyal and loving friends, of which Susie is one. In the name of Jesus, I'm honored, Amen.

A Mother's Memories

"Mom!" Joshua hiked up his pants.

Joshua walked home from afternoon kindergarten with his siblings. No doubt this conversation would be about his britches slip-sliding once again.

"What? And how was school today?"

His face scrunched in agony. "You've got to help me. This belt does not keep these jeans from falling."

I sat on the couch and wiggled my finger for him to come nearer. "Let's see." Observing his midsection, I came to a conclusion. The child's hips were too narrow to hold his britches in place.

My mind churned with a plan. "What if I were to make your pants? I would custom-fit them to your build."

His eyes twinkled. "Well, sure."

After material and pattern shopping, I sewed a pair of denim slacks to fit him perfectly. He didn't need a belt, but he wore one to look nice for school.

"Thank you, Mom." Joshua hugged me. "No more yanking up my jeans."

Later, I bought bigger-sized patterns of the same design to continue making Joshua's slacks as he grew. He wore custom-fitted pants until the summer before he entered sixth grade, when he decided he wanted store-bought jeans like his friends.

I was a little sad I would no longer be making them for my grown-up boy. And yes, he still pulled up his britches, even with a belt, and I was still needed to cut and hem his pant legs.

Those were happy moments for Joshua and me, dear Father. The relief on his face for wearing slacks which fit made it worth the extra work. Through Jesus's holy name, Amen.

~Your Mother Memories~

~Your Prayer of Praise~

~A Scripture of Encouragement~

FORTY-EIGHT: First Anniversary after Joshua's Death

He will cover you with his pinions, and under his wings you will find refuge.

—Psalm 91:4

"My son supported your decision not to abort your baby?"

We were at the reception after the first anniversary memorial of Joshua's passing. Many of Joshua's closest guy friends from high school, members of *The Crew*, attended with a few of *The Crew* girls.

Oh, how they had grown into fine adults.

As *The Crew* sat clustered along the lawn, as they once had in high school, I told them one day I would write Joshua's story and they would be in it.

Some smiled. A few nodded. Many wore sorrowful expressions. One young man cried.

My tears came, also, standing before the broken-hearted young people who loved my son.

Several asked me the question his family still asked: Why did Josh do it?

I told them his pain became unbearable, so maybe this was why. One *Crew* member said he didn't know Joshua was ill.

A young lady, one of Joshua's closest female friends, came up to me after *The Crew* disbanded. "I have something important to tell you."

Tears pooled in her eyes.

I hooked my elbow in hers. "Let's go over here to talk."

"I'm so sorry for your loss."

Now, she stood in front of me, wringing her fingers. "Joshua was such a good guy." She touched my hand.

"You need to know he supported my decision not to abort my baby."

After I gasped, she continued. "Because the father abandoned me, I was undecided as to what to do. Joshua stood by me, and it helped me to make the decision to keep her. And I'm a Christian now because we studied the Bible together during my pregnancy."

Conversation finished, we hugged and cried, wetting each other's shoulders.

"Thank you, honey," I said, "for telling me the rest of the story about your baby."

Holy Father. I'm deeply grateful this woman stepped forward to share this about my son. It makes me appreciate Joshua even more. Please bless the child who is now a young adult. In Jesus, Amen.

A Mother's Memories

Eighteen-year-old Joshua came in late on this particular evening.

"Mom, can I tell you something which is a secret?"

Swiveling in my office chair, I faced him. "Sure."

"My friend is pregnant."

I took off my glasses. "Did you tell her to come see me at the crisis center?"

"Yeah, I did."

"Son, I'll meet her at Lifeline even if it's my day off."

"I'll tell her." And Joshua nodded.

Joshua's friend didn't come into the pregnancy center. But often, Joshua spent time with her or they chatted on the phone. Soon enough, Joshua told me she was keeping her baby.

At the time, I thought he meant she decided not to release her baby for adoption.

After Joshua's friend delivered her child, she moved away and never saw him again.

Thank You, Father, I'm glad my son was a support to this young mother. Through Christ, Amen.

~Your Mother Memories~

~Your Prayer of Praise~

~A Scripture of Encouragement~

FORTY-NINE: Burying Joshua's Ashes

I can do all things through Christ which strengtheneth me.
—Philippians 4:13 KJV

I pushed the dirt in the deep, dark hole, where it splat, splattered onto Joshua's urn. "I don't feel strong."

My sister-in-law had just told me I was the strongest person she'd ever known—as she knelt beside me and helped cover Joshua's urn.

A few minutes before, no one had moved after the prayer.

No one reached for the shovel to cover Joshua's ashes.

Jami had wrapped his urn in a soft cloth, and the urn was laid in its resting place. Then, the small crowd stood still.

All was silent, except for the sniffing and blowing of noses.

Not a procrastinator, I dropped to my knees and scooped dirt with my hands.

Someone said to me in an anxious voice, "We have a shovel."

Guiding more dirt to where it had to go, I said firmly, "No. I'll do this."

Others above me wept.

With my sister-in-law on her knees to my right, another relative dropped down to my left.

He pushed the dug up ground with us. And as I wailed, he patted my back with his other hand.

The three of us moved the fresh pile onto the remains of our beloved.

Oh, Lord, the love of family. In Jesus's holiness, I rest, Amen.

A Mother's Memories

"I don't want to die." Joshua's statement set off the events of a two-hour discussion.

Minutes earlier and at midnight, Joshua had locked our front door behind him and went into the garage. In his own words, "It's like I woke up from a daze, realizing I was about to kill myself."

At one point in the conversation, Joshua shook his Bible. "We don't realize Who we're dealing with."

He said, "When I was a child, Bible classes did not prepare me for adult life. People shouldn't candy-coat the Bible to their children, for they need to know all things about God."

Then, at two a.m., Joshua locked himself in the garage with a gun.

On the other side of the door, I spoke in a calm voice. "Joshua, you need to let me in." A long eternity of silence, and I cringed.

"Come on, Son, it's late and you're tired." *Please don't shoot.*

After what seemed light-years, Joshua opened the door. He was standing by the washing machine with a towel over an arm, and his other hand hid inside the towel.

"Can't a guy do his laundry?"

"It's too late for that." I walked over to him and wiggled my fingers. "Let's go, Son."

Certain his weapons were out of his reach, I stayed awake on suicide watch. At eight a.m., I made phone calls to get Joshua in to see a therapist.

When I couldn't get a doctor appointment for this day, I called our insurance company and told them Joshua was suicidal. They agreed to allow Joshua to see whoever would take him immediately.

A concerned therapist said he would rearrange his schedule and see Joshua at one o'clock. We had time to eat and get ready.

I breathed a sigh of gratitude. Surely, God had answered our urgent prayers during this long morning. Help was an hour away.

But, our son said good-bye when he handed me his Bible.

Oh, God, will we ever know why? In agony, I ask You through the name of Jesus, Amen.

~Your Mother Memories~

~Your Prayer of Praise~

~A Scripture of Encouragement~

FIFTY: The Morning after Joshua's Burial

But the Spirit entered into me and set me on my feet, and he spoke with me and said to me, "Go, shut yourself within your house."
—Ezekiel 3:24

The next morning after we buried Joshua's ashes, I walked into the living room after waking.

Something was different within me. Lighter. It seemed a boulder had rolled off of my shoulders and scales fell from my eyes.

I didn't want to bury Joshua's urn. Instead, I wanted it to sit upon my fireplace mantel forever.

But now I sensed it was the right decision after all.

Standing at an end table, I swiped my fingers across the wood surface. I did the same to the entertainment center.

"All this dust."

Thinking hard, I couldn't recall dusting in over a year. Too preoccupied with my grief work, it was not important.

Right then I remembered again what *The Compassionate Friends* lady said to me at the park all those months ago.

"Jean, plow through the middle of grief. Do not turn left or right or you could become lost. And when you successfully come through to the other end, you'll have more compassion for others who've lost as you have lost."

Wanting to believe her, I took her advice.

I would have never made it without the kindness of others. All of them sent by You, Lord, at the perfect moment, including Your Son. In the comfort of Jesus, Amen.

A Mother's Memories

"Mom, please don't go." Joshua and I stood outside in the backyard the day before I was to leave for the weekend.

I placed my fists on my hips. "Do you know what you're saying? I've waited a year for this trip." Joshua averted his gaze.

Two weeks before his death, Joshua's fears had become extreme: contamination of our drinking water and the air we breathed. He was convinced our house swarmed with toxins from the central heating. His arthritis pain increasing, this could be part of the reason why Joshua grew paranoid.

Now, I peered closer at Joshua in hopes he would look at me. "What's wrong, Son?"

"I'm not feeling quite like myself." Joshua sucked in a deep breath. "I don't want to be left alone," he said on the exhale.

Joshua's chest heaved and his lashes fluttered, and I blinked. "Okay, I won't go."

Walking toward the house, my selfish side hurt for the loss of a much-wanted getaway. I had planned to work on a children's nonfiction book project in my motel room. But the closer I got to the back door, an alarm blared through my head. In recent weeks, Joshua had stopped talking to us. Now he confided?

This mother's heart knew all was not right. In this precise moment, I sensed a shift within our lives. I couldn't name it or image it, but whatever it was couldn't be ignored.

The next day, we were playing Scrabble. During Joshua's turn to make a word, I brought in bed sheets from the dryer. Sitting on the floor across from him, I wrapped myself within the sheets. Warmth enveloped me, and I stopped shivering.

Joshua let out a boisterous laugh, startling me. Since he had been in such a down-trodden mood the day before, I didn't know what to say.

"You." He pointed. "You're silly-looking in the sheets."

I frowned, but was glad for a more normal moment in our otherwise quiet game.

"I wouldn't be doing this if you'd let me shut the windows and turn on the heat. It's thirty degrees, Son."

Joshua shook his head and buttoned his lips. I stared at him in disbelief for he had ground my nerves to powder.

Lord God, this was a low point for us as family. Did I fail Joshua, Lord? But, how could I have known his erratic behavior meant something as serious as death? Please, Father, clear up my confusion. In Jesus's holy name, I ask, Amen.

~Your Mother Memories~

~Your Prayer of Praise~

~A Scripture of Encouragement~

FIFTY-ONE: I Miss Joshua 24/7

Let us therefore, as many as be perfect, be thus minded: and if in anything ye be otherwise minded, God shall reveal even this unto you.

—Philippians 3:15 KJV

Even though it was midnight, I inserted a Jesus movie into the DVD player, and lay on the sofa.

For a moment I forgot about loss and pain and focused on Jesus Christ. My heart swooned with love for Him, and His willingness to die for us. For me.

After the movie ended, I clicked it off and the screen went blank. Then, I remembered. No Joshua. No reason to live. When will my tears dry for more than a day? When will my heart stop hurting—beating?

You can mend my shattered soul, Lord. The miracle of this? Even in my present wretched state of mind, Jesus loved me.

I opened my eyes and gazed at a wrought-iron Scripture plaque on the opposite wall. I had recently bought it at a Bible bookstore. It read: Joshua 24:15: *But as for me and my house, we will serve the Lord.*

Out loud, I said to my Lord, "I miss Joshua 24/7." The moment those words left my lips, a stirring moved within me.

I waited and listened.

Was the Holy Spirit telling me to read Joshua 24:7?

I leapt off the sofa and retrieved my King James Bible. I flipped the pages and was reading Joshua 24:7. A sinking feeling grew in my heart—until the very last part.

And there it was: *And ye dwelt in the wilderness a long season.*

What's this?

Understanding came to me. "Oh, Lord, no!" Not me suffering with agonizing grief for a long season. Not me still in this house. Not me in this detested wilderness wandering.

Rereading the verse, I hoped I had misunderstood. But no.

Afterward, as I lay there, silent tears rolled along the sides of my face and dripped, dripped into my ears. I allowed God's Words to soak over my soul. A growing sense of awe replaced disappointment.

God gave me a message. He had woven another blessing through this mother's heart.

Holy Lord, I do not like the idea of a longer season. But You are God, and I'm not. In the love of Jesus, Amen.

A Mother's Memories

Within weeks after our son's original memorial service, a mother of one of Joshua's friends sent me a paper.

It was a writing assignment completed by Joshua's third-grade class.

The mother knew I would enjoy this paper titled "I Would Like to Have the Gift of . . ."

The note inside the envelope stated she thought I already had it, but sent it just in case. But, Joshua had never shared this with me.

Below are a few examples of what Joshua's classmates wrote (names withheld for privacy):

"I would like to have the gift of a whole bunch of people knowing I care about them. If I had this gift, I'd feel really happy. I would feel wonderful." —girl student

"I would like to have the gift of courage. If I had this gift I'd jump. I would feel terrific." —boy student

"I would like to have the gift of love, happiness, and the gift of the Holy Bible, Jesus, God. If I had this gift, I would spread it. I would feel wonderful." —Joshua Williams

Joshua's words doubled me over, and I wept.

Oh, God, I hate this loss! What happened to this beautiful child? People who knew Joshua well, said it best.

"Joshua bore more pain and sorrow in his twenty-five years than many people do in their long lifetime."

Life caved in on my son.

Father God, my innocent son's words showed me he had been listening to our bedtime Bible stories of so long ago. And, the logical side of me understands I did not fail my son. In Christ's name, I thank You for another blessed gift, Amen.

~Your Mother Memories~

~Your Prayer of Praise~

~A Scripture of Encouragement~

A Note to Readers

Dear Reader,

Thank you from my heart to yours for taking the time to read this true account after the loss of my son.

It has been over a decade since Joshua died by suicide. What I have learned so far is God will never leave me. Bad things happen, but it does not mean God forsakes us in the difficulty.

As I've shown within these pages, the Lord has woven blessings through my heart to *ease* the sorrow.

Living in the house for four more years after Joshua's death was next to the hardest after the loss of him. Believing God made a horrific mistake, I had many serious talks with Him.

And I asked often, "Why, God, are You making me stay in the home where Joshua died?"

It's a true saying God's timing is always perfect, and before someone bought our home, God allowed me to teeter on the edge.

One night I was tempted to join Joshua in death. However, something stopped me from killing myself. This is called Love. God's Love.

After I chose Love, I lay in my bed exhausted and sobbed until dawn. Stubborn parts of me emptied with each teardrop and soaked my pillow, as I surrendered my broken heart to the Father of Love.

I understood, He could then begin the reshaping process of making me the woman God has wanted—me needing Him for everything.

I now pray without ceasing—meaning throughout my days. It's not only a want to, but a need.

Over the years, what has become easier is the grieving, though I still ache for my son, Joshua.

When I wake each morning someone special is missing, and yet, when I rise, I count the blessings God has given to me while I meet Him with a prayer on my lips.

A hope in my heart.

God bless you, dear mother, as you walk this journey and choose to come through on the other side with a God-given stronger spirit.

In Him, Jean

"Sometimes fear does not subside and one must choose to do it afraid."

~ Elisabeth Elliot

About the Author

Jean Ann Williams is a member of American Christian Fiction Writers, and Society of Children's Book Writers and Illustrators. She has contributed articles on suicide loss at www.opentohope.com, and currently for *Putting on the New* blog, and her own *Love Truth* blog.

Jean Ann and her husband live on one acre in Southern Oregon where they raise a garden, fruit orchard, goats, and chickens. Her favorite hobbies are hiking through the woods, practicing archery with her bow, and big game hunting. Their two remaining children have blessed them with thirteen grandchildren, their baker's dozen.

To contact Jean Ann, please visit her website at www.jeanannwilliamsauthor.com or her blog at www.joshua-mom.blogspot.com/.

If you enjoyed this book, please consider leaving a review on Amazon, Goodreads, or by word of mouth. Thank you.

Suggested Reading

David Cox & Candy Arrington. *AFTERSHOCK: HELP, HOPE, and HEALING IN THE WAKE of SUICIDE.* Nashville, Tennessee, B&H: Broadman & Holman Publishers.

- This book offers a process of what to expect after a suicide loss with encouragement.

Margaret Brownley & Haiku by Diantha Ain. *Grieving God's Way.* Enumclaw, WA, WinePress Publishing.

- Inspirational with beautiful Haiku for those who seek truth through God.

Marilyn Willett Heavilin. *Roses in December: Comfort for the Grieving Heart.* Eugene, Oregon, H: Harvest House Publishers.

- A personal account of one woman's faith and struggle after the loss of three sons.

Grief Sites:
www.allianceofhope.org
www.compassionatefriends.org
www.facesofsuicide.com
www.forevermissed.com
www.griefnet.org
www.griefshare.org
www.hopeline.com
www.opentohope.com
http://www.pos-ffos.com
www.virtual-memorials.com

Made in the USA
Middletown, DE
16 November 2019

78843941R00116